MORE
RESCUE
Smiles

BEST-LOVED ANIMAL TALES
OF RESILIENCE & REDEMPTION

EDITED BY **TAMIRA THAYNE**

Published by Who Chains You Publishing
P.O. Box 581
Amissville, VA 20106
www.WhoChainsYou.com

ISBN-13: 978-1-946044-32-7

Printed in the United States of America

First Edition

To all those who have rescued an animal
when you could have walked away.
We thank and appreciate you.

Also from Who Chains You Books

ଓଓ

Rescue Smiles: Favorite Animal
Stories of Love and Liberation

Foster Doggie Insanity: Tips and Tales to Keep your Kool
as a Doggie Foster Parent

A Doggie Hero is Born

The Chained Gods Series

The Puppy Who Left Puddles on the Floor

It's About A Dog

The Second Chance Series

If Your Tears Were Human

The Kindness to Animals Series

The Dog Thief and Other Stories

The "Our Side" Collection

The Animal Protectors Series

The Muffin Series

And Many More! Visit us at WhoChainsYou.Com

Contents

A CERTIFIED ASSISTANCE SETTER:
Clancy's Triumph

BY DARLA PURGASON

MY FUTURE PARTNER WAS ON DEATH ROW at the Culpeper Pound in Virginia when Larry Spivak of Irish Setter Rescue pulled him out and give him another chance at life. I named him Clancy—a good Irish name for a good Irish lad!

"Oh, he's a good dog," most people said, but they didn't

1

think he could become an assistance dog.

It's funny; I never had a doubt.

I didn't know how my multiple sclerosis would affect me from one day to the next. Furthermore, the loneliness which resulted from not being able to keep up with others was edging me ever closer to depression.

The Girl Scouts taught me to be prepared, so I was determined to train an assistance dog while I was still on my feet. It was the logical thing to do, but my heart insisted on an Irish Setter.

Clancy approached training as he did everything else—he was easy going, but with a touch of blarney. At first I couldn't get used to the fact that he didn't purr. His total, slave-like devotion made me feel bossy, telling him to "sit" or "stay".

I was used to cats; you don't tell them anything. He wasn't used to cats—he thought they must taste like chicken. So in our house, leaving the cat alone became his first lesson. Once he understood that the short, fat, furry fellow was part of the pack, he never bothered with him again.

Clancy already knew the basics, so he breezed through obedience, while I struggled with the commands and signals. We continued his training at Amy Tester's establishment, Just For Dogs, in Alexandria, Virginia. She would give us homework and we would go home and practice.

Clancy was a good pupil until it came time to retrieve. He would actually sit on the object and look around as if to say, "Pick up what…where?" For two months, we had a war of wills, until finally he just couldn't stand this nagging woman any longer. He began to half-heartedly pick up the items I requested and sort of fling them at me.

Metal objects presented the biggest challenge. The night

he picked up my car keys, I broke down in tears. Clancy took his final and passed with flying colors.

Working every day in Washington, D.C. is no easy task for any dog, but Clancy soon became known as "the Mayor of 14th Street." Strangers would pass us and say, "Hi, Clancy!" I color-coordinated his uniforms, leashes, and collars so he always looked professional. He would actually prance down the sidewalk, picking up his front feet like a Clydesdale.

Construction noise, traffic, even packed elevators didn't faze him. The isolation I had felt dissolved as people came up to talk with me while we walked during our lunch break. Exercise is an important part of my therapy. Clancy and I saw parts of the city that I didn't know existed and wouldn't have felt safe to explore if it hadn't been for my new partner by my side.

One day during our lunch-hour walk, I decided to brush up on his training. A squirrel skipped across the sidewalk in front of us. "Leave it," I said. As we turned the corner, a pigeon landed directly in our path. "Leave it," I said again. Finally, as we walked up 15th Street heading for home, a young, shirtless Marine in shorts ran past us, sweat glistening down his back, muscles rippling. Honestly, if Clancy could have talked, at that point he would have been the one telling me to "leave it!"

After just a few months of on-the-job-experience, we were invited to the White House to see the Christmas decorations. I was a wee bit apprehensive—after all, it was THE WHITE HOUSE! The only embarrassing part was when they confiscated the pepper spray I had in my purse. The Secret Service just loved Clancy, and understood my explanation about needing backup protection.

It was really crowded inside as we walked from room to room, gazing at the decorations. Clancy was on his best behavior despite the chaos, and he delighted the nearby children by picking up my cane for me when I dropped it.

Working dogs are constantly surrounded by hazards. When you least expect it, things happen. Wednesday evening was my time to visit the chiropractor, but no one mentioned that Santa Claus would be arriving at the same time. We walked into a room with wall-to-wall children, and the commotion that comes with it. Not knowing what else to do, I took a seat to wait my turn.

The child beside me was scrambling out of her coat. As her mother spun her around to extract her other arm, she came face to face with Clancy. Without hesitation, she took her forefinger and thumb and soundly beeped him square on the nose! I sat there, stunned, but Clancy, eyes dancing, merely smiled, like he was saying "Back 'atcha, babe."

Crowded subway cars were another challenge. Some people don't hold on, so a sudden stop or change in speed can result in a large person falling on an unsuspecting dog. The potential for even small injuries like a stepped-on foot or a pinched tail kept me alert.

One evening, a gentleman was holding onto the strap directly above my head. His other hand held a heavy, black briefcase which dangled by his side, just in front of Clancy's face. The man gazed out the window, totally oblivious to his surroundings. I tugged gently on his coat until he looked down at me. I smiled, pointed to Clancy, and said "Just in case he decides to lick your hand, I didn't want you to think it was me."

Within a matter of years came the first event I had

planned for when adopting Clancy. On Christmas Day, the entire right side of my body went numb. It was as if someone had drawn a line from the top of my head and down the center of my body. Luckily for me, disability allowed me to stay home while I underwent steroid treatments.

Nothing could have prepared me, though, for how I would feel emotionally. Clancy helped me up the stairs to bed, stayed by my side during the two-hour IV drips, and—most importantly—he was there to keep me company during the steroid-crazed nights when I couldn't sleep.

I finally returned to work, and Clancy helped to bring me back to health by walking with me until I was my old self once more. We continued working together for years, until old age and ill health forced me to retire my best friend. Now, it became my turn to watch out for him, to help him when he stumbled, to pick him up when he fell.

Who would have thought that this homeless dog would go on to have such a splendid career? Clancy served as a shining example of a certified assistance dog; his attitude defined the word "friend".

Although I miss Clancy every day, I know he's waiting patiently for me at the Rainbow Bridge; of that, I have no doubt.

ॐॐ

Darla Purgason is retired from her work in Washington, D.C., and keeps busy with cat rescue endeavors as well as caring for her own four beloved long-haired kitties. She enjoys trying new vegetarian recipes, listening to books on tape, and doing embroidery. She is the author of *A "Tail" of Two Christmases*, and makes her home in Culpeper, Virginia.

ONE IN A BILLION
Tallulah's Tale

BY HEATHER LEUGHMYER

WHEN YOU'RE AN ANIMAL RESCUER, you are often the first person to come to mind when there's an animal in need—and the type of animal doesn't seem to matter. I had been rescuing rats for a few years and had gotten to know various people at some of the local animal shelters when a call came in about a stray pig.

The woman on the phone was someone I had met at a shelter in a nearby town during a large rat rescue, who also happened to be vegetarian. "Animal control brought in a pig today," she said. "They found this girl wandering down a road, and they said if no one takes her they are going to give her to a farmer to raise for slaughter; I don't want that to happen. Do you know anyone who could take her?"

I didn't, but being vegan myself, I was determined to find someone who could. I wasn't about to let her become pork chops or bacon.

I began to research farm sanctuaries online and that's when I came across SASHA Farm. SASHA Farm stands for Sanctuary And Safe Haven for Animals, and is located in Manchester, Michigan. I called the number on the website in hopes that someone would answer and they would have room for a pig. I tried not to get my hopes up too high, because when you are involved in the day-to-day work of animal rescue, you quickly learn that there are always more animals than homes or safe places for them to go.

Often, animals must be turned away due to lack of space or funds—a sad and brutal reality of the rescue world. A woman named Dorothy answered the phone, and I had gotten past my first hurdle. I told her what I was calling about, and asked if they had room for another pig.

I was pleasantly surprised when she said that the sanctuary would take her! When I got off the phone I was elated, and quickly called the shelter back to tell them I'd be driving the pig to a sanctuary, where she could live out the rest of her days.

The next morning, I arrived at the shelter to pick up the rogue pig. She was loaded, much to her dismay, into a large carrier, and let us know she was unhappy by squealing at the top of her lungs. She was no bigger than a medium-sized dog at the time, but she seemed to believe she was fighting for her life.

Her ears had been notched and her tail had been cropped—signs that she had come from a large factory farm. The ears of the pigs are notched for identification purposes, and the tails are cut off to deter tail-biting in overcrowded conditions. These painful mutilations are always done without anesthesia, so it's little wonder she had a distrust for humans and protested what we were doing to her.

Once she was inside the crate and loaded into the vehicle, she calmed down, burrowed under her blanket, and went to sleep. During the two-and-a-half hour drive from Warsaw, Indiana to Manchester, Michigan, she would wake up periodically for treats and then burrow under the blanket again for another nap. I would talk to her quietly, and eventually she seemed to realize that we were not going to hurt her and that she was finally safe.

I'm pretty sure I even saw her smile.

When we arrived at the farm, we were greeted by a man named Monty, who helped unload her into her own stall filled with fresh hay and straw. She was timid at first and didn't seem to know what to think of it all, but she quickly made herself at home by rooting in the hay and making herself a comfy bed.

I kept in touch with the owners of the farm after that and learned that they had named her "Tallulah." Tallulah quickly became a farm favorite due to her social and gentle nature. At least once each year I would visit her and all the other animals who live happily at this beautiful and peaceful place.

There, each animal has value beyond their "use" to man, and they are treated with compassion and respect. People come to SASHA Farm from all over to meet animals who were once abused or neglected and viewed as mere commodities, and yet who have learned to trust and love once again in spite of their previous treatment at the hands of humans. Each animal has a story to tell and a lesson to teach. SASHA Farm, and others sanctuaries like it, are places where compassionate people can come together to celebrate the lives of all beings.

Tallulah lived out her life at SASHA Farm without ever having to worry about being treated cruelly or ending up on someone's plate. Here, she was able to feel the sun on her face, breathe in the fresh air, and take mud baths under blue skies on warm summer days. This is the life she and others were meant to live, and somehow fate allowed her this wonderful gift.

Out of the billions of others who are bred and raised only to be slaughtered at a very young age, who are mutilated and confined and denied everything that is natural to them, she was one of the lucky few. Tallulah passed away when she was 10 years old. Due to the way she was bred, her legs became lame under the weight of her body, and she could no longer walk. She crossed the rainbow bridge peacefully, surrounded by those who loved her, and she will never be forgotten.

Today, SASHA Farm continues to rescue and rehabilitate farmed animals who might not have anywhere else to go. Each year, festivals are held in order to allow the public to mingle with these amazing beings so they can see for themselves the individual personality each animal possesses and the endearing quirks that makes each one unique. The resilience it takes to overcome the abuse and/or neglect many of these animals suffered and to be able to love and trust again is awe-inspiring. Humans have so much to learn from these intelligent and emotional creatures—if only we would take the time to truly see them for the beautiful, feeling beings they are, and to listen a little closer to our consciences and our hearts.

Smile, Tallulah

On a country road you sit alone,
Confused by passing cars.
Ears notched, tail cropped, someone's property,
Yet somehow, here you are.

Born into an industry
that sells you off for parts,
You must have seen the darkness—
Humans without hearts.

Did you sense your mother's sorrow
Before this fateful day?
Did you look into her desperate eyes
As you were ripped away?

Did you see her tiny prison?
The boredom she endured?
Did depression overwhelm you
With every cry you heard?

You sit outside the shadows now,
But what about the others?
Where are your suffering sisters?
Where are your brutalized brothers?

You're just one among billions,
Your life somehow spared—
Now you're given a chance
To find humans who care.

A lost little miracle,
You have so much to teach—
So many minds to change.
So many hearts to reach.

You're special, Tallulah,
And now you're on your way
To a place you only dreamed about
To live out all your days.

Your worried face grows more relaxed
And with every passing mile
Your pain and fear begin to fade
And I think I see a smile…

Smile, Tallulah, smile.

ᘒᘓ

Heather Leughmyer is the author of *Adopting Adele, Brave Benny, Courageous Conner, A Rat's Guide to Owning a Human, If Your Tears Were Human,* and co-editor of *Rescue Smiles.* She is also the founder of Happy Endings Rat Rescue, and a graduate of Indiana-Purdue University with a B.A. in Writing and Linguistics.

Writing has been a passion of hers for as long as she has advocated for animals. She lives in Columbia City, Indiana, with her husband, daughter, and several animal companions.

WHAT WOULD DAISY DO?
Daisy Mae's Lessons in Love

BY LAURIE LEE

A FEW YEARS AGO, I WAS HELPING a very dear friend of mine move her sister, Kay. I didn't know Kay very well, but my friend asked if I would be able to spare some time to help, so I told her I'd be glad to go along.

Kay had been renting a very secluded cabin in northern Wisconsin. We had just finished loading the rest of the boxes and were ready to leave, when Kay mentioned that she was glad to be leaving this too-secluded area—except that she'd be sad to leave the wild dog she had been feeding.

I was shocked and needed to know more. "What wild dog?" I questioned.

She told me that she'd been putting bowls of food and scraps behind the garage, and a feral dog would come out of the woods to eat it, and then promptly slink back into hiding again. The dog would never allow her to approach, escaping if she got too near.

Except, Kay told me, when she would leave the house and pull out of the driveway—then the dog would hurtle out of the woods and chase her down, only retreating if she stopped the car to attempt interaction with her.

Luckily we were three cars strong, so I told them I had to try to rescue the dog. I simply couldn't stand the thought of her left all alone out there, starving and lonely. I assured them I would follow very soon, but I needed to stay and see what I could do first.

After some discussion and urgings on their part to leave with them, they went ahead and departed. Sure enough, as they drove out the gravel lane, a very thin, tan dog ran out of the forest and chased the cars down the driveway.

My mission was on! I had some snacks with me, so I tried to lure the dog out, but to no avail; she disappeared into the woods and I could not find her. No amount of pleading helped, and I felt like I was at the end of my rope.

This went on for hours, and by now it was getting dark. I had no plan and was several hours from home.

I hunkered down next to my vehicle and starting crying; once I got started I couldn't stop, so I sat there and cried and cried. After about twenty minutes of this I looked up, and the dog was standing by my side!

She then let me pick her up and put her in my car, and I just couldn't believe it was happening—I felt like I was in a dream or something. How could this be real?

Yet it was.

I had done it. I'd rescued her…or had she rescued me?

I already had two dogs of my own, and had no intention of keeping the dog I would later name Daisy Mae. That all changed when we got home; I saw the way my dogs welcomed her, and I remembered the joy she had already given me by coming to my side when I thought all was lost. I just couldn't deny her a place in my household, for I loved her already and I never wanted her to feel alone and hungry again.

Daisy would prove to be one of the kindest, wisest dogs I have ever met. In just one example of her big heart, one of my girlfriends was leaving an abusive boyfriend, and found refuge at our home for the night. We put my friend to bed and closed the door, but Daisy must have known there were tears being shed, and helped in the way only she knew how.

In the morning we awoke to find every dog toy in the house in front of the guest bedroom door—and there were many; she even included a baby blanket from her bed. When we saw what she'd done, how'd she'd tried to help my friend, there were even more tears and hugs, as Daisy had once again managed to touch the hearts of all who met her.

I was blessed to have Daisy as part of my family for 15 years, and I will always consider her to be one of the finest gifts I have ever received.

In hindsight, it was my tears that drew her to me that day so many years ago, and her compassion for me had in return saved that skeletal, timid dog from a sad and uncertain future. Her loving nature had allowed her to get past her own fear to minister to a hurting human.

Daisy Mae had proven to be a beacon of light in a world which greatly needed it. Her lessons in love still guide my actions today.

ჯ

Laurie Lee hails from Wisconsin, where she learned the joy of dogs from her mom and dad. It was her favorite part of childhood. In those days it wasn't called "rescue"; instead her mom and her girlfriends were known as "the crazy dog ladies" and her house became known as "the dog house". Today Laurie is two dogs strong, but is leaving the door open to one day again adopt a third.

MY GIRLS, MY RESCUERS
Zora, Annabel Lee, and Havana

BY SIDNEY DuBOIS

EACH OF MY CATS HAS COME TO ME in a different way, and each time I rescued one of them I believed in my heart that I was saving them. Yet, over the last few years I have came to realize that this is not the case at all—they were, instead, saving me.

I was diagnosed with anxiety and depression at the beginning of my college career, and, at first, this diagnosis didn't mean much to me. Everyone has anxiety, right? The problem was that I didn't understand the extent to which these challenges would play a role in my daily life. The resulting despondency began to dictate the things I did or didn't do or participate in on a regular basis.

During my sophomore year, most of my family moved from Ohio to North Carolina. This was hard for me, but I was determined to deal with it, push on through. At the same time, my grandfather became extremely ill from cancer. I had recently lost both grandmothers, and it felt like loss was surrounding my life.

I had been considering taking a medical leave from school. The college noticed that my grades were fine, but I had stopped socializing and leaving my room. I had stopped getting out of bed, was constantly calling off work, wasn't showering, and wasn't eating.

This behavior just wasn't normal for someone in college. Any time I tried to talk to my friends about what was happening with me, I would end up instead feeling cast out and shut down because they didn't understand how I felt. They heard what I was saying, and it concerned them because they had been told if someone says these things you should seek help, but they didn't know what to do or say to me. Here I was seeking help, I was on medication, but yet something was missing.

Over Christmas break I decided that maybe I needed out of Ohio for a little while. Maybe it was the weather, maybe it was the people around me, or maybe I just needed my family. I wasn't really sure what it was, but I knew staying at school wasn't a very good choice, and staying with my remaining family in Ohio wasn't the best choice either.

So I packed my bags, and after my last class I headed south. I quickly found that December in Ohio is much different from December on the ocean in North Carolina. The weather is warmer, and I was beginning to feel more like myself again; yet there were still times when I struggled. During one of my talks with my mother, she suggested that I visit the local shelter, so I decided to take her up on it.

To be honest, I really wasn't sure that this was something I wanted to do. I worried one of two things would happen: I would fall in love with an animal I couldn't have, or I would feel sadder because there were all these animals who didn't have homes. But I went anyway.

I had lived with animal companions for as long as I could remember. Not having a four-legged friend at school had bothered me, but I had seen them when I visited my parents, so I believed that I was fine. Apparently, it bothered me more than I had realized.

When I got to the humane society, the first thing I did was visit the various cat rooms. The way the shelter had it set up was amazing. Cats were grouped by age and the rooms smelled very clean. The cats were not put into cages, and provided they got along well with others, they could roam as they pleased.

I went from room to room. A kitten was way too much energy for me. I needed a cat who was more laid back—one with some spirit but who mostly just wanted to hang around.

All the cats were adorable and made me smile, but when I came to the "teenage" cat room, I saw a little grey cat who was shy and off by herself. There wasn't much to her at all. She came over to me, and it didn't take long for me to notice that she was a clumsy little girl. She virtually fell over her own feet as she made her way across the room to me. She had these massive green eyes that were too big for her head, her ears were large, and she was definitely the clumsiest cat I'd ever seen. The kittens had more grace than she did.

I picked her up and she made a little huffing noise as if to say, "Really, you're going to pick me up?" I began to ask questions about her. She was a Russian Blue, which meant very little to me; she had been there a year and a half, she really was not that social, and as far as they knew she had a bad start after being dumped in a cardboard box on the shelter steps.

I stroked her for a little while, and then made up my mind that it was time to leave. I went home and told my mom about the awkward little cat that was reportedly always getting her claws stuck in toys, but I didn't ask to get her. I tried not to think about her for a few more days into my trip.

Then I decided I wanted to visit her again. Really, I had thought that she would be gone, but she wasn't. I picked her up and cuddled her every time I was there, and each time I wanted her more and more.

Eventually I couldn't take it anymore, and decided to ask both Mom in North Carolina and Dad in Ohio if I could get her for Christmas. My parents discussed it and I applied to adopt her. I really felt I had no hope of getting her, especially when I found out a home inspection was involved.

I was so anxious I could have vomited. I spent the next day looking at litter boxes, cat toys, a cat crate, litter, food, bowls, and anything else I felt I might need for this little grey cat. My stomach sank though, because I still worried that I had no chance of adopting her—at least not before I was supposed to go home.

The day before I was set to leave my phone rang; when I answered, it turned out to be the shelter—I was approved to come pick her up and take her home with me! It felt so surreal.

It was the happiest I had been in a very long time. I drove to the shelter and officially adopted her right then. I didn't know just how much we would go through together, and what she would mean to me then. I felt like I was saving her, and that was a wonderful feeling.

I brought her home with no clue what I was going to name her. I thought about it and thought about it, but still nothing came to mind. Finally, I began pondering some of my favorite authors.

I thought of those whose books had meant something to me at one point or another. I settled on naming the little grey cat Zora—after Zora Neale Hurston. I had read about some of her struggles while I was in high school, and I related very deeply to her written words. Sometimes when I felt down I would think of her or another author and remember that these women had made it though their struggles—so could I.

Hurston is a southern author, and it seemed fitting that even though my cat wasn't from Florida, she was still from the south. I brought her home and we've pretty much been together ever since. Zora later qualified to be my ESA (Emotional Support Animal) at my school.

She stays with me when I cannot find the motivation to get out of bed, and gives me that motivation because she needs me. I cannot lay there all day, because she must be fed and watered and cared for. Because of the feeding routine I have with her, she lets me know when she's hungry or if I'm late with dinner. She will paw and meow at me.

When I'm sick or just having a day where the bed feels like the best place for me, she will stay by my side. Often, I can find her under the blankets and snuggled right next to me. She follows me to the shower and sometimes sits at the edge of the tub—maybe she thinks I need feline supervision.

We have been together for almost three years now, and I can honestly say it doesn't feel nearly that long . . . and it will never be long enough.

Zora Gets a Sister

About a year after I got Zora I noticed she started to act lonely and a little different. I wondered if I should get another cat to keep her company. Another cat really wouldn't be a problem for me, because once you have one you have all the needed supplies for a second. I looked around a little, and felt that a kitten would be best because she could adjust to another cat a little better if we had him or her from a baby. I didn't look very hard though; unfortunately, kittens are all over the place in Ohio, and typically it isn't hard to find one. I just hadn't come across one that I felt would be a good match for Zora yet.

My brother soon found a very small, grey kitten and began sending me pictures. She was cute, but it was clear she was also very sick. I wasn't convinced the kitten was ready to be away from her mother either, because she seemed so tiny.

When the kittens were eight weeks old, I set up a time and date to meet with the person who had them and the mother at his house. When I saw her condition with my own eyes, I was shocked. I refused to even think of a name for her, because I was sure that she would have some sort of illness such as feline leukemia, or she would die from something else any day now—she was that unhealthy. She was overrun with fleas, had worms, an upper respiratory infection, an eye infection, and ear mites so bad they were all the way to the edges of her ears.

In my mind, there was no way this kitten was going to make it. When I got her to the vet they asked for a name, so I explained that she didn't have one and why she didn't have one. After looking at her, they clearly held the same opinion as I did.

The testing and treating began. All of her bloodwork came back clean, and I was surprised. The vet warned me that she probably wouldn't make it through the night—she only weighed .74 pounds! I gave her a bath in the sink because her litter mates had urinated and pooped all over her, and I couldn't handle the smell anymore. The water that came off her ran red. There was flea dirt, and dried blood, and who knows what else in the water.

When she was clean and dry I had to bottle-feed her, which was something new for me to learn and quickly master, as her life depended on it. Once she was fed I placed her on the bed next to me, and Zora curled up in her normal spot behind my knees, paying little attention to the tiny grey ball of fluff. Somehow she survived that first night, and I just kept caring for her as one day led into the next.

The routine of feeding the kitten and putting her in my hoodie pocket continued for about a week before I noticed a big difference. All the medication and care seemed to finally be paying off. That's when I decided I should name her.

I called her Annabel Lee, because "Annabel Lee" by Edgar Allen Poe is one of my favorite poems. After several weeks of antibiotics, several rounds of deworming, and multiple ear mite treatments, she became a fairly healthy kitten whose quirky personality quickly shone through.

Today Annabel Lee weighs in at almost ten pounds, is on special diet food, and comes with her own anxieties. She follows me around the house with a consistent thud as her paws hit the floor. She purrs on my chest, comforting me, when I am watching TV or reading a book.

Annabelle Lee and Zora may not be cuddly or touchy-feely with one another, but they have no idea what to do when the other is gone, and will look around the house until they've found each other again. Zora is the boss, but Annabel Lee has become the companion Zora needed.

The Unplanned Feline

 I began working at the animal shelter during my final years of college, and discovered it's not easy to keep from falling in love with every cute little critter that comes through the doors. Some of them are lucky and are adopted quickly, while others have to wait for a good home, and through no fault of their own could be there for months, even years.

I have seen animals who are clear cut abuse cases, and yet somehow they turn out to make the best pets. I have seen others who appear to be untrainable, only to find that they become the most gentle, loving animals with a little work and guidance. When I met Havana, she was a little black ball of fur, huddling in the back of her cage and refusing to come out for anything in the world.

Her big, yellow eyes shown brightly against her black fur, which was dull and falling out due to severe anxiety and stress. I could see that she had not had an easy road of it, but I had no idea just how bad that road had been until much later.

I was working at the shelter several days a week, along with my sister, all throughout that summer. Havana refused to come out of her cage for at least a month. Every day I would leave the door open, letting her decide whether to venture forth or not. One day she finally did; however, she stayed in a corner of the room, away from the other cats and all by herself. If anyone came close she would run back to her cage and return to huddling.

Finally came the day I was able to coax her over to me. I petted her and showed her that I would not hurt her. I was determined by then that if no one took her, she was going to come home with me. I just wasn't sure how to make that work yet.

After a few days of her allowing me to get close to her, I noticed her mouth had something weird going on with it. I opened her mouth and saw that one of her front teeth was turned all the way up toward the roof of her mouth. This impertinence on my part earned me a good smack on the head, and a hiss for good measure.

Havana went flying back to her cage and refused to come out again that day. I began to notice little marks all over her head, back, and other parts of her body. Someone had really done a number on this poor little cat. I started to ask questions about where she had come from and what had happened to her, but didn't get many concrete answers.

One day we were holding an adoption event, and I was really hoping she would get a home. I found out that she was supposed to be shown, but as a barn cat and not as a family member. This did not sit well with me.

To be clear: I do believe there are some feral cats who can do well in that kind of situation, as long as they have the skills needed to survive. However, in was my opinion that this particular little cat did not.

In that moment I decided to adopt her myself. I called my dad and talked to him about it, and as I suspected, he was furious with me. I had already brought home three rescued cats and a dog by this point, and we were all full at the inn. Eventually he agreed to let me have her, on the condition that I stopped volunteering.

I took her home that day.

She spent at least a week hiding from everyone, and was not eating very well. Once she started to get to know Zora and Annabel Lee, however, she decided that maybe she would be ok there. I couldn't get too close to her at first, because my large size compared to hers felt too scary to her. Eventually, though, Havana began to see that no one in our home would hurt her, and she started coming out and interacting more and more.

I took her to the vet and found out the extent of the abuse that had happened to her before she came to the shelter. The tooth I had seen in her mouth had been twisted around multiple times with a pair of pliers, she had had something shoved in her ears (possibly even a tool such as a screwdriver), her tail and ribs had been broken, and her microchip had been forcibly removed.

I never really expected her to fully trust me after all that. But she turned a year in February, and has come so far since her adoption. She actually plays now! She still doesn't know what to think of some of her toys, but her favorite ones are furry and soft, and she carries them in her mouth or bats them down the hallway.

She chases Annabel Lee all through the house, and Zora perches up high and watches them. Havana crawls in bed with us too now, making sure to claim her share of the cuddles. For a cat who—I was told—would never be affectionate or find a home, she has exceeded all expectations, and become a very loving girl.

In fact, Havana has a ritual she follows: she headbutts me multiple times, purring while doing so, then licks my face and chirps. Yes, she chirps.

She follows me all over like a shadow. Her fur has come back, and has grown in nice and thick.

These three girls have brought me so much happiness. They have become the reason I get up in the morning, and they inspire me to go to classes and to work. They remind me that I have to take care of myself, because they need someone to take care of them.

I talk to them every day about my challenges, because they are not going to tell my secrets or hurt me. They listen and don't judge me—even if they DO occasionally look like they are.

It took me a few years to realize that, while I had believed all along that I was saving them, it was actually just the opposite, and these three girls had saved me instead. Without them I really don't know where I would be today.

But because of them, I'm not only surviving, I'm thriving.

ॐ

Sidney DuBois recently moved from Ohio to North Carolina after graduating college with a B.A. in Education Studies and English; she is currently working towards her masters in Special Education. She has researched and studied various ways in which companion animals can act as therapy for children in reading programs or other forms of therapy.

HE WAS AN OAS SURVIVOR
Alex Comes Home

BY RON SMITH

IT WAS APRIL OF 2013, and a post from "OAS–Life Inside the Sanctuary" appeared on my Facebook news feed. After reading the post and doing some research on the Olympic Animal Sanctuary (OAS) in Forks, Washington, it appeared to me that the 125 (or more) dogs that were crammed into cages in an old warehouse were being neglected and needed help. So I contacted the administrators of the Facebook page and offered to get involved in whatever way was needed.

As I continued to research the Olympic Animal Sanctuary and what was taking place behind closed doors, I came across an OAS promotional video on YouTube titled, "Alex: Off the Chain." As I watched the footage, I was appalled to see Steve Markwell, founder of the sanctuary, scaring poor Alex and forcing him into a dog crate.

Later in the video, Markwell mentioned that Alex would be up for adoption soon. Markwell's cell phone number was listed as a contact number on the OAS website, so I immediately called him. He didn't answer, but I left a detailed message offering to adopt Alex.

When I got no response, I placed several more calls to Markwell over the next week; he never answered the phone and never responded to any of the voicemail messages I left. It seemed apparent that he wasn't interested in allowing me to adopt Alex.

After I got nowhere with my adoption attempts, I contacted Pati Winn, one of the "OAS—Life Inside the Sanctuary" Facebook page administrators. I told her I wanted Alex, and if there was any possible way she could get him out of that situation, I would gladly drive to Washington state from California and pick him up as fast as I could get there.

Pati assured me that if anything changed and she had a chance to get Alex out of there, she would do so and hold him for me. I'd done all I could do.

As the summer of 2013 dragged on, virtually no progress was made toward freeing the OAS dogs from that awful pink warehouse in Forks. I often wondered, and worried, if something bad had happened to Alex, or if he was even still at OAS. The silence was frustrating.

After months of exasperation, Jeff Bernside from KOMO-TV in Seattle aired the "Sanctuary of Sorrow" story on the evening news. He went out to the sanctuary and spoke to Markwell, but neither he nor his cameras were allowed inside the building. The pressure on the Olympic Animal Sanctuary and its founder Steve Markwell immediately increased due to the negative news coverage.

In November and December, protestors marched through the town and demonstrated in front of the sanctuary. Hundreds of calls from concerned citizens were being made to the City of Forks, demanding that they shut down OAS. A few days before Christmas, Steve Markwell loaded all the dogs into a semi-trailer and disappeared.

A few days later Guardians of Rescue announced that Markwell was enroute to an undisclosed location, and would be turning the dogs over to their nonprofit organization. I, as well many others in the rescue community, breathed a sigh of relief.

Guardians of Rescue obtained possession of the dogs in

Golden Valley, Arizona, and began to list the dogs' names on Facebook as they were taken off Markwell's truck.

I was so excited! Right away I started planning, even before I knew if Alex had made it to Arizona. *I can drive the 750 miles and back, no problem,* I said to myself. But as I watched many of the dogs' names scroll across my screen, Alex's name had not been listed yet. . .

As you can imagine, the OAS drama and misinformation about which dogs were there and which weren't quickly took over the internet, and—to my knowledge, at least—Alex had not made it to Arizona. I was heartbroken.

Then I got an unexpected phone call one afternoon. The woman said, "Is this Ron?" After I affirmed that I was indeed the man in question, she asked, "Are you the person who wants Alex from OAS?"

Wary now, I hesitantly said, "Yes." What was going on here?

The caller told me, "I'm on my way to Golden Valley to pick him up and bring him to you."

My first thought was, is this a scam? Instead, I replied, "Alex hasn't been listed as arriving in Golden Valley."

The caller, Pat Webb from Wheels 4 Paws Transportation, assured me. "He IS there and he's fine, actually; I've been asked to pick him up and drive him your way." I was almost in shock and disbelief. After a few more minutes of conversation with Pat, we made arrangements to have her bring Alex to Redding, California, to meet me.

A short time later, another call came through about Alex. This time it was someone from the rescue group, who asked in an urgent tone, "Please tell me you have a fax machine?"

"I DO have a fax machine, actually!"

"Good. I'll fax you the adoption paperwork for Alex. Please fill it out ASAP and get the pages faxed back to me this afternoon. Can you do that?"

Mere moments later, she'd sent me the files, and I hurriedly signed everything and faxed it all back to her.

It suddenly struck me what I'd done: I'd just made arrangements to adopt a large German Shepherd and have him delivered to my house! If Alex had really lived outside on a chain his whole life before ending up in a cage at the sanctuary, as Markwell claimed, he might be a wild or vicious dog. He certainly would not come house-trained. Uh oh.

But I was so happy that Alex was alive and free, something I'd feared was not the case, that I didn't even care. I would deal with whatever happened when he got here.

Alex was FREE! And he was going to be my companion. I couldn't wait.

Pat delivered Alex to my house on January 3, 2014, just as we'd arranged. When I first met Alex, he was afraid and not at all friendly. Pat was very patient, thought, and helped us both feel more comfortable with each other before she left.

From the first moment Alex stepped foot into my house, it was very evident that he had not spent his whole life on a chain, as Markwell had claimed in his video. He was a perfect gentleman inside our home, and had been trained to stay off the furniture. He also knew basic commands and was housebroken.

The first couple of months with Alex and I were a bit trying. I had to give him a lot of "No Bark" training, and he would react in an aggressive, fear-based manner when he encountered anyone who was unfamiliar to him. As time passed, thought, he became less afraid, he barked a lot less, and his temperament improved. To this day he remains distrustful of strangers, and will warn them off if they get too close to him.

Today, Alex loves to go on walks and relax in the back yard. Sometimes he does a little digging, and he even did one major excavation job on what used to be the lawn. He does enjoy his time outdoors, and to be able to run without a chain jerking him backward, but he lives inside with me and mostly stays right by my side, where he belongs.

Alex and I are greatly appreciative of everyone who helped save the OAS dogs, and who brought us together as a family. I felt from the first time I saw him in that video that he was meant to be my companion, and I have not a regret in the world about the way things turned out. Alex ended up in a great home and I ended up with a best friend who doubles as an amazing watch dog.

⟡

Ron Smith was born in Southern Oregon, but his family moved to Shasta County, California when he was a baby; he has made Shasta County his home ever since. In the 1970's, Ron began managing and investing in residential rental property, which he does today after retiring from 40 years in the transportation industry.

Publisher's Note: If you're interested in reading more about the OAS rescue, *I Once Was Lost, But Now I'm Found: Daisy and the Olympic Animal Sanctuary Rescue* is also available from Who Chains You Publishing.

FROM SUFFERING TO SANCTUARY
The Livingston Eight

BY BRECE CLARK

HAVE YOU EVER GOTTEN A PHONE CALL and knew your life would never be the same? It was Friday, September 29, 2017, when SASHA Farm Animal Sanctuary received just such a call. On the other end of the line was the Livingston County Sheriff's Department, and they were asking for help with animals at a small Michigan dairy farm in the county.

The animals were reportedly living in a filthy environment, and were in poor body condition. Many had died due to starvation and thirst, and their bodies were left where they'd fallen. After repeated failed attempts to contact the owner of the farm, the sheriff's department obtained a search and seizure warrant to remove the animals. Could SASHA Farm help?

Our answer, of course, was a resounding "Yes!"

Exposure of animal cruelty on modern factory farms, whether for meat, eggs or dairy, has long been documented by animal rights groups and concerned citizens. Even the standard government-stamped-approved practices such as mutilation of infant piglets, forcibly impregnating female cows, or gassing male baby chicks alive are enough to make even the most insensitive person weak in the stomach.

Many of those who do not support the above methods often argue that such conditions and systems don't exist on small farms. In this case, at least, they would be wrong.

Arriving at the dairy farm, a passerby would never have suspected unusual or neglectful conditions. The property was located on a back country road, with a large white farmhouse overlooking a series of red barns. The yard was adorned with expensive farm equipment and one could imagine that this once represented the iconic American dairy farm.

The further we traveled onto the property, however, the more the signs of abandonment became apparent. It was as if we'd entered a ghost town. There were no signs of life—no happy animals running around, no farmer whistling merrily on a tractor. We saw only dilapidated barns, sheds with broken windows, and overgrown weeds. There was an eerie sense of despondence.

Attached to a rundown building full of equipment was a

make-shift pen, which was patched together with rusty gates and broken boards. Inside the pen was a rancid mixture of mud, manure, and urine nearly three feet deep. There, standing in waste up to their knees, were four emaciated cows. These were the animals we'd been called to rescue.

Their bodies were so ravaged by dehydration and lack of food that they looked like Auschwitz prisoners. Bones protruded through their skin, eyes were sunken into their skulls, and feces was caked all over their frail, deteriorating bodies. It was clear that these poor creatures hadn't been fed for weeks. After recovering from the shock of such a scene, we simply burst into tears on behalf of these trapped animals.

There was just one water trough available, which held only a few inches of slimy, green water. Perhaps the most frustrating and heartbreaking thing of all, though, was that directly across from these dying animals was a barn full of hay.

Someone simply had not cared enough to feed them.

We acted quickly and devised a plan to remove them from this hell hole and get them to safety. The rescue was difficult on so many levels, but like countless times before, SASHA Farm Animal Sanctuary did what we had to do to save these cows.

As we trudged through the knee-high pit of waste, our boots filled with feces and we nearly got stuck ourselves. It took everything we had to corral the cows onto our trailer, but finally they were loaded and their lives had already changed for the better—at last they were free.

Before leaving we heard grunting noises nearby. We fol-lowed the sounds through an old barn packed with junk and debris, and discovered three 2-month-old piglets stuck in a dark corner. Their pen was four-sided and solid, offering no sunlight or fresh air. They, like the emaciated cows, were standing in so much urine and feces that the smell nearly knocked us over. Within minutes, we were able to pull them too from their dark dungeon of existence.

Once the three little pigs were tucked safely away in the trailer with the cows, we looked at each other with heavy hearts and sighed deeply. So much suffering, so much abuse. And for what? Why? How could mankind be so cruel?

At least seven lives had been spared, we told ourselves. At least their suffering was over. Still, our hearts broke for all those we hadn't been able to save.

As we were about to drive away, one of the sheriff's deputies asked if we could visit another property that was owned by the same farmer. They weren't sure how many animals (if any) had been abandoned there, but neighbors had become suspicious and the officers felt that it was worth visiting—especially given the circumstances here.

With the four emaciated cows and three little pigs in tow, we held our breath in dread as we pulled up to the second farm just a few miles away. Upon first glance it appeared not much different than the first; a traditional 1900's style farm. Exploring the property further, however, we found that the main barn had a chain locked around its front doors. We feared the worst but knew we had to get inside in case there were animals trapped in there.

As we took a bolt cutter to the lock and slid the doors open, nothing on earth could have prepared us for what we would find.

There before us, littering the floor of this old barn, were

seemingly countless dead cows. At the sight, we broke down in tears. We cried openly for these poor animals; we cried for their misery, their neglect, and their torture. We felt devastated and utterly helpless. We knew, though, that our pain was nothing compared to the pain and suffering that the animals before us felt during their slow and torturous deaths.

Scanning the area further, in a side corner of the barn, we couldn't believe our eyes when we came upon a sole survivor. Standing solemnly among the remains of his former herd mates and family members was one black and white cow. His body was ravaged from hunger. Bones protruded and dried feces covered his entire body. One could barely identify this animal as a living being. Had he been lying down, we could have easily mistaken him for one of the dead.

Encouraging him onto the trailer was not easy. His body was so weak that he couldn't even step up. We took our time though, gave him some of the first food he'd had in weeks, and eventually managed to get him inside. Peering into the trailer we saw a helpless victim—an innocent animal who had done nothing to deserve this.

We grieved hard. With tears in our eyes we promised him and the others that they would never again know such pain and suffering. Only kindness would enter their lives from now on. We promised them a safe, comfortable, happy life with us at SASHA Farm Animal Sanctuary.

The five cows and three piglets are doing well now. It's been months since they were rescued from that horrible situation; all have been treated by a veterinarian and are on the road to recovery. The cows have their own private barn

where they receive a plentiful supply of food each day, clean
water, and access to twenty acres of rolling hills pasture.

Initially they were afraid and mistrusting of us, under-
standably so, but as time goes by they are learning that not
all humans are bad. A few have even become comfortable
with head scratches.

The three little piglets have been introduced to our other
pig residents; everyone gets along well and enjoys their large
barn and three acres of pasture. They are so full of energy
and charisma that it's a joy for us just to watch them. They
seem to have overcome their fear of humans quickly, and
now regularly ask for belly rubs and ear scratches. At night,
all three of them sleep side by side under the comfort and
coziness of a straw bed.

If there is anything to be learned from this experience,
we hope that the public is made more aware of the condi-

tions for animals on farms everywhere. Many of the same cruel practices that are exposed on large farms happen on the smaller farms as well. Regardless of the size of the farm, problems exist when animals are viewed as property and/or products in general.

Animals are individuals with an interest in living. Like us, they seek love, comfort and companionship. When we use them either for food, clothing, or entertainment, their lives become diminished, a means to an end. The people who owned these farms treated the animals as though they were mere property, and then abandoned them to a certain death.

Although the Livingston Eight finally got their happily-ever-after, the pain they suffered to get there is unacceptable in today's society.

SASHA Farm Animal Sanctuary is the largest farm animal sanctuary in the Midwest and is home to over 250 residents. To learn more about their work or to donate, visit their website at www.sashafarm.org.

✥

Brece Clark is a dedicated animal rights advocate and Humane Educator. Brece grew up on a small dairy farm in Mid-Michigan and was a professional horse trainer for many years. His passion for animals has evolved over the years, changing from a perspective of exploitation and use to one of liberation and compassion. Brece's voice for animals has been heard around the country with organizations like Animal Equality and the Humane Society, but he now focuses his activism with SASHA Farm Animal Sanctuary. Brece has also begun to share his personal experience and perspective as a professional horse trainer with local audiences speaking as The Humane Cowboy.

Photo credit for all images this story: Cassie Pietron and Chase VanEckoute.

ECHOES OF THE
Rescue Walls

BY THALIA DUNN

IF THESE WHITE-WASHED CINDER BLOCKS
uttered a sound,
what would it be? What could it be?
An echo of the sounds the walls surround?

Clatter of dog food pouring into metal dishes;
squeaky faucets as water bowls refilled.

Commands quickly given,
calming words whispered,
as volunteers tend to
the abandoned and afraid.

If these walls echoed the sounds,
what could we hear?

Meows of a hungry tabby, who lost her way
now in a metal cage; anxiously licking her paws,
waiting for her guardian to retrieve her.

Whimpers of a black lab puppy, lonely, confused,
rejected because his owner could not appreciate
his protective barking in the night.

Frantic yaps of a tiny pug shivering in the corner,
against the lonely cries and angry howls he hears.

Panting, sniffing of a tired terrier,
picked up on the country road
wishing he could get home after he chased squirrels
too far from his familiar world.

Quiet purrs of a scrawny feral
curled around a metal food bowl
as he lazily swipes kibble with an easy snap of the paw.

Cheers of ecstatic volunteers when another rescue
bounds out pulling at his leash,
new family members beaming behind.

As barks, meows, whimpers, and growls echo off the walls
filling the air with mournful longing,
we'd hear the collective plea,
"I don't belong here.
Take
me
home."

If these cinder block walls could talk,
what would they whisper to those they shelter?

"Hush, little puppy, your new family is coming soon
to take you home, where you will sleep in a cozy dog bed
and grow with a freckled faced toddler
who will love you forever."

"Take heart, old chap,
I know you're confused

that your owner dumped you here.
Your new friend will choose you
because of your greying muzzle and kind eyes.
Trust your new home
will be perfect for you to grow old in."

"Keep going" the walls would encourage tired workers.
"We'll stand strong, not crumble,
but protect as you provide
for these forgotten creatures
who yearn to be loved."

For the walls talk and absorb
and echo the sounds
of all that they surround.

Thalia Dunn currently resides in New Jersey. She is an aspiring poet
and writer of short stories dealing with the themes of the natural world,
animals, and cycles of life. She is also a storyteller for children's groups
and, to pay the bills, teaches in a local high school.

LESSONS LEARNED
Zander Girl

BY STEPHEN PLYLER

ZANDER GIRL'S STORY IS IMPOSSIBLE TO TELL without talking about the reason for her rescue. My calling to rescue was always loud and clear—passed on from my parents as a kid, then cemented by a natural ability to understand the behavior of our canine friends.

What wasn't as clear early on in my rescue life was my call to rescue feral dogs. The first feral was Maggie, then several personal rescues followed, and soon countless others at the shelters that I volunteered for. Somewhere along the way I saw the need for someone who understood them; someone who loved an animal who was not capable of loving them back—someone with the unnatural human ability to be able to set aside the need for reciprocal love.

Thus began my dedication to feral dogs and my mission to educate the public about their plight. They are the forgotten ones. Born of domestic dogs in the wild, they miss human contact during the formative part of their early lives—the socialization window of the first four months. This leaves them living as wild animals, struggling to survive in a world that sees them as a threat. Often, they lead short, painful lives. It's survival of the fittest. These dogs are the first to be euthanized at the shelters, feared and misunderstood.

That brings us to Doyle. Doyle was the leader of a feral pack in east Texas, a pack which was being cared for to the best of her ability by a local woman. Doyle was a dog who was so feral that he would not even approach a human when food was present, staying far back in the distance while his pack ate, and getting only leftovers after the human was gone.

Doyle was brought into my pack over two years ago, and at first it was slow going with him. He was comfortable in his safe spots and bonded with me, though he was scared to death of new experiences and being outside. He was loved by everyone who got to know him for his crazy hair styles and his quirky personality.

When you adopt or rehab a feral, you undertake an obligation like you've never experienced with another dog. You quickly come to understand that you are solely responsible for keeping the dog safe and secure at all times. Because of their instincts, these pups don't understand what is best for them or even what they want.

The nature of a feral dog can be confounding and confusing, a challenge to the heart and soul of both parties. For myself, I look back at the day the worst happened and second guess everything I did. I failed to keep him safe. The gate latch broke, and the wind blew open the gate. Doyle followed the other dogs out but then he panicked. In an instant, he was gone.

There he was, in a new area that he didn't know, disoriented and lost. The search that followed is well chronicled. It was a brutal game of hope and disappointment that tore asunder my ability to understand this fleeting game called life.

Finally, we received what we hoped was a good tip. It was Super Bowl night when we got a call from a lady who lived an hour south of us, near Santa Fe. She said there was a small, terrified, wire-haired dog living under her deck who matched Doyle's description. I was supposed to be going out of town to Texas the next morning, but this might be Doyle! He had to come first.

So, instead, I armed myself with a humane trap and headed south to see if she truly had Doyle. When I got there I realized this would not be an easy task. This deck was huge at 60'×40', and it sat very close to the ground, leaving very little space under it to see or maneuver. As the Super Bowl went on inside, I was competing in my own contest outside—sledge-hammering apart an old deck with rusty screws and rotting wood. Not surprisingly, the husband of the well-intentioned lady was not too thrilled about us breaking apart his deck, but I would deal with that dilemma next.

I baited the trap and started to drive home, but was concerned about the temperatures that night and the dangers that this dog (Doyle, I hoped) could face spending the night in the trap. I decided instead to stay close by, and asked the woman to check the trap before she went to bed. Exhausted from the day's events, I tucked myself into bed at a local Casino's hotel.

Around midnight she called. We had trapped the dog! I jumped out of bed and quickly drove over to her house. Was this Doyle? The five-minute drive to her home seemed like an eternity. My hope was soaring, but then like so many times before, it all came crashing down. It wasn't Doyle!

I'm not sure what I thought I was going to do if it wasn't Doyle, but now I was faced with the reality to which I hadn't given much consideration. It was now after midnight, and there sat a scared, feral dog—that wasn't mine—trapped in my cage. The lady thanked me for trapping the dog and said she was sorry that it didn't turn out to be Doyle. She asked if I could leave the trap, because the dog could stay there through the night and then she would take him or her to the shelter in the morning.

Even though I was feeling sad about Doyle, I knew what I had to do. Odds were good that a very unsocial/feral dog would not survive at the shelter, and it was going to be 10 degrees that night. I couldn't let this poor dog stay out there in that cage all night. I thanked her for her help and said I would be happy to take responsibility for the dog.

What transpired next played out like a Hollywood comedy script. I now had a feral dog in a cage in the back of my covered pick-up truck, and I needed to get him or her into a NO DOGS ALLOWED hotel. There was no way I would be able to sneak a large trap inside without being noticed. I would need to wrestle this wild dog out of the trap and into a crate that I could carry in.

Let's just say, if you have never done such a thing while squatting in the back of covered pick-up truck, it's not as fun as it sounds. But that was only part of the challenge. Next, I had to sneak the crate past the front desk and several intoxicated gamblers in the hotel lobby. I'm not sure if anyone saw me, or if they just figured they had drank too much, but at least I made it to my room without being accosted. Whew!

I'm not sure what prompted me to make the next decision, but I lived long enough to regret it. Maybe I was fooled by her (yes it turned out to be a girl) seemingly docile, less-than-feral-actions the following morning, because I decided to take the feral dog on a five-day Texas road trip with me! Looking back, presumably it wasn't the best idea I'd ever had.

What followed included explosive diarrhea, a 45-minute midnight howling session, a fear-induced bite to my neck, and several adorable moments of her finding herself in the mirror. I named her "Zander Girl", after Doyle Alexander, because without my search for him I'd have never found her. I knew at that point she needed me as much as I needed her.

Although I was in denial for a little while, I eventually acknowledged that she was going to be a forever dog. When fate talks, you listen, and I have no doubt that Zander Girl was brought here to help me forgive myself for my failure with Doyle.

We are now several months into her domestication, and Zander Girl is no longer the scared, semi-feral dog that huddled in the corner of a cage on Super Bowl night. She is a goofy, fun, loving light that illuminates every part of my broken heart. The loss of Doyle still haunts me, but I can't help but think about what would have happened to Zander Girl if it wasn't for Doyle. And when I think about that, for a moment my heart heals just a little, and I can forgive myself for not always protecting him.

So I guess that is the lesson Zander Girl taught me: you don't ever replace a loss, but sometimes you can learn to forgive yourself. And sometimes, by loving another, you love yourself again too.

Lesson learned, Zander Girl.

ᏬᏬᎧ

Stephen Plyler was raised in a family with more dogs than people; he has always loved animals. After a brief flirtation with teaching, Stephen found his calling as owner of The Antique Gallery LLC, the largest Antique Mall chain in the U.S. His successful business has allowed him to enjoy other passions: he has worked with bears, started a radio station, been a music producer, promoter, and award-winning radio personality, and is currently mastering the art of photography. The love of his life has always been his family, which includes his partner of 24 years, Jeff Trammel, their 11 rescue dogs, and their turtle named Bud. These days you can find him hiking the mountains and living the dream in Bend, Oregon.

OUTFOXED BY A KITTEN
The Unforgettable Felix

BY PAUL ERNEST

MY CHILDHOOD RESCUE OF A KITTEN named Felix would turn out to be one of my most memorable, at least of those that took place during my "salad years"—when I was green with inexperience.

I discovered Felix along a boat-docking wharf which was adjacent to the parking lot of a hospital. I had broken my left leg in a soccer game several weeks before, and my mother and I were just coming out of the hospital on a Friday evening from yet another round of physical therapy.

As we entered the back parking lot, we heard a commotion at the far end of the property. "What's going on?" I asked, turning toward my mother.

Just then I heard her gasp. "It's a kitten!"

And so it was: a little tabby-and-white kitten, dashing (actually, he was more like bounding, tiny-kitten-style) across the asphalt.

Meanwhile, a bunch of decidedly lower specimens of humanity were laughing, throwing stones, and joking about cooking and eating the little feline.

I took off after the kitten, hobbling as fast as I could and ignoring my mother's calls of "Paul! Your leg! Don't run!"

I chased him under one of the parked cars, then I got down on the ground, reached under the vehicle, and grabbed ahold of him, hauling him out and into my arms. (Mind you, this was no simple feat with a stiff, atrophied leg.)

I then carried him past his astonished tormentors and over to our car. His attackers were evidently so stunned that they didn't do or say anything to me, and I had no trouble from them as I walked to the safety of my mother's vehicle.

She was standing by the driver's side door with her eyes wide and terrified, but her relief was palpable when she saw me safely approaching. "Get in, let's go," were her only words, and I moved as fast as I could, definitely onboard with that idea as well.

We set off for home with the kitten on my lap, purring and sucking on one of my shirt buttons. (As the super-glue ads say, "bonds within seconds.") Of course, he wasn't the only one who bonded all too readily, and I was immediately convinced that I wanted the little guy to be part of my family, too.

As we were driving, I got the lecture I was expecting: "We have too many cats already. This one will make nine. Your father will be very angry. We can't keep him; he's got to go to the shelter."

Our local SPCA (a kill shelter back then) was on an on-ramp by the freeway, and it was rush hour, so my mother said to me, "Now I have to watch traffic, so I want you to look for an opening to pull into the SPCA lot."

"Ok," I said, ever the dutiful son. Then I, in the front passenger's seat with the kitten still batting at my buttons, saw an opening in the crush of traffic—and exercised my right to remain silent.

We subsequently missed the turn, leaving my mother no choice but to abandon her immediate plan to drop him at the shelter, and instead take the kitten home for the weekend until the SPCA opened again on Monday.

This "fortunate happenstance" gave Felix 48 hours to charm my parents, and I'm happy to report that he succeeded admirably. By Sunday night, I overheard my mother musing, "He really is cute, isn't he? Maybe we should just keep him."

To help matters along, we also had a motherly orange cat named Sheba who decided Felix was her long-lost kitten; she washed him, played with him, and protected him from the other cats. Given his small size when found (he barely weighed a single pound), I credit Sheba with playing a big part in saving his life.

By the end of that weekend, Felix had managed to

ensconce himself as a firm member of our swelling human and animal family. All talk of the SPCA vanished, and we settled in to have a good many wonderful years together.

I think we were both a little proud of ourselves.

☙❧

Paul Ernest is an editor for a legal reference publisher, and volunteers as a prosecutorial assistant and legal researcher for the Animal Legal Defense Fund. He shares his Texas home with two dogs, Sandy (a toy poodle), and Chica (a chihuahua).

TSETHAR, THE PRACTICE OF LIFE RELEASE
Orchid, Susan, Flower, and Piute

BY SUSAN HARTLAND

"Nothing is more precious than life itself
And no negative act more serious than taking life.
Therefore, among composite forms of the roots of virtue,
None has greater benefit
Than the ransom and release of animals.
If you wish for happiness and good fortune,
Be diligent on this supreme path..."
—CHADRAL RINPOCHE

TSETHAR IS A TIBETAN WORD—Phóng Sanh is the Vietnamese equivalent—often translated as "life release". It is the Buddhist practice of saving the lives of animals who are destined to be killed. For wild animals, this can mean releasing them into their native habitats, and allowing them to live out their days as nature intends.

For domesticated animals—or for wild animals who cannot for whatever reason be rehabilitated to the extent that release is possible—this would mean that these animals live out their lives in sanctuary, where the utmost care is taken to provide them safety and as much freedom as logistics can grant.

Even for those who consider every life precious, it is impossible to get through life without causing suffering to even a single being. Doing harm is part of this experience called living, and we can all think of ways we've unintentionally caused suffering to those who share our planet.

In Buddhism, the consequences of karma—intentional action—are sometimes portrayed as a balance, with one side of the scale measuring acts of kindness versus a person's unfortunate deeds on the other. Following this method of reasoning, it becomes possible to counteract the damage we all do by intentionally performing good deeds—like giving the gift of life to another.

The Buddha taught that saving the life of another being is the most beneficial action we can take, and some of his followers have expanded upon these teachings. Buddhist Master Nagarjuna said that "Saving Life" is the highest of all virtuous activity, and Buddhist teacher Hungkar Rinpoche believes that meditation on love and compassion means to give up, as much as we are able, causing harm to other beings.

The practice of "life release" usually involves the purchase of an animal directly from a slaughterhouse or fisherman, often on auspicious days in the Buddhist calendar. The animals are then blessed before being returned to their natural environment, with prayers often dedicated to someone who is ill or has died in the belief that that person too will benefit from this dedication.

Of course one does not need to be Buddhist to adopt this practice, and most westerners will forgo the religious rituals and ignore the self-serving component of compassion for which the original tsethar custom has been noted. Knowing the animal is safe and the feeling of satisfaction that comes from doing good is for most of us reward enough.

In the animal welfare and rights movement of today in the U.S., tsethar has become all about animal liberation.

In our country, buying an animal's freedom is often controversial; when you buy a lobster from a restaurant or grocery store to release it into the ocean, pay fishermen to release their catch of fish, or purchase domesticated animals from the factory farming industry, it can be argued that you are simply paying for the replacement of the animals you are trying to save.

A liberationist performing tsethar therefore should always ask him- or herself the following question: am I acting as a rescuer, or simply as a customer?

Every individual and every sanctuary has to make his or her own life decisions and choices, compassionately but rationally, and then act from that inner conviction.

The concept of tsethar was foreign to me, but I recently had my first experience with the practice while working as executive director at the Wildlife Waystation, a nonprofit organization in Angeles County, California. During my tenure with the sanctuary, I was instrumental in rescuing and finding placement for five horses whose lives and freedom were bought out of compassion and a genuine desire to give them a chance at a life worth living.

The founder of Wildlife Waystation, Martine Colette, has in her 40+ years of existence taken in more than 77,000 abused, abandoned, orphaned, and injured animals at her California sanctuary. Often these animals were relinquished by private owners who couldn't care for them anymore, had become "obsolete" in laboratories or the entertainment industry, had been impounded in raids, or for other varied reasons could not be released back into the wild.

Although Wildlife Waystation is by its very mission a wild and exotic animal sanctuary, it has throughout its history taken in domesticated animals in need when dire circumstances warranted it.

Historically speaking, here in the U.S., horses are not raised for food. However, they are often dumped at auction houses by people who no longer can—or care to—provide for them, or when they are no longer needed for exploitation by humans (such as racing, working, or premarin lab equines).

Horses headed for slaughter often include even pregnant mares and foals, which most would agree is particularly heinous. According to the American Society for the Prevention of Cruelty to Animals, the data from 2012 to 2016 shows that an average of 137,000 American horses are trucked over the U.S. borders to slaughter facilities in Mexico and Canada every year, and are often butchered for human consumption in other areas of the world.

Fortunately, though, the last three U.S. slaughterhouses—two in Texas and one in Illinois, all foreign-owned—were closed in 2007. Even when these facilities were still in operation, tens of thousands of American horses were exported to other countries for slaughter.

The horses who end up at U.S. auctions, through no fault of their own, are looking at a very grim future without the intervention of rescuers and activists. At these auctions, rescuers can save horses by outbidding the kill buyers; the auction house and/or former "owners" make money, of course, but there is no automatic replacement of the rescued horses—making for a stronger case on behalf of those who pay for these beings' salvation.

The first horse I "rescued" remotely from an auction house in Texas, I learned about through a network of rescuers who work to save equines slated for slaughter. My friend Lisa Agabian was part of this group, and kept many of us abreast of the plight of the horses at U.S. auction houses.

The horses are sold off relatively inexpensively, but finding donors or rescuers who can not only afford the animal but the cost of the long-term care is difficult. On one day in particular, I was following the auction process and in contact with the rescuers on the auction floor. There was one horse left to be saved, and the price for her freedom was $400.00—a mere pittance of her worth, but still a lot of money for me.

Even though I lived on a non-profit salary, I decided I would save this animal, because I knew that my friend and the founder of the sanctuary I worked at would help me find a place for her. I went online and set up an account and tried to purchase her, but my card was declined.

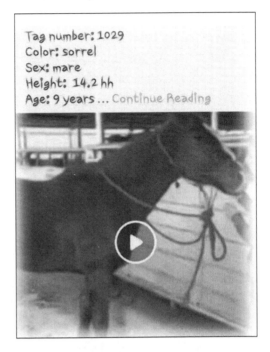

Tag number: 1029
Color: sorrel
Sex: mare
Height: 14.2 hh
Age: 9 years ... Continue Reading

The bank had apparently seen a purchase to an animal auction house and questioned it, taking it for a fake transaction. I was under the gun, because in a very short time this poor girl would literally be forced onto a transport truck to a slaughterhouse. I grabbed my bag, let the staff know I would be offsite for an hour, and drove the 10 miles to my nearest bank branch. I stood in line for what felt like forever while the horse's minutes ticked away.

I begged the teller to fix my card so that I could use it; she called the manager over, and we repeated the same discussion, with me explaining that it was literally a life and death situation. They were finally persuaded to reset the card, I sent the funds successfully, and she was pulled at the last moment.

Whew! I was never so relieved, and felt incredibly lucky that one of the most stressful hours of my life at least came with a positive outcome.

That hurdle passed, I now had to find someplace for her to go. The team on the ground had a temporary spot to shelter her, and since she was in Texas and I was in California, I had to trust their judgment.

Within a short time, these same rescuers that pulled her found her placement on a farm outside of Houston that helped elderly people, and they would provide transport for her to get there and ensure it was a good situation.

Normally, I would never relinquish an animal without personally seeing where she was going, but I believed these women were committed to saving these animals and giving them the peaceful years they deserved, so I hoped for the best and sent the horse I would never see a silent blessing for a wonderful life.

The next auction rescue I was involved in was for four horses who had been saved from another Texas auction floor by a woman named Suzy. Suzy had pulled the four that day with the promise that they would have a home at a California ranch. The horses were put onto a trailer and headed west to their new home. When they got there, however, the situation was not as promised, and Suzy was not comfortable leaving them there. But what was she to do now?

Scrambling, she messaged me and asked if Wildlife Waystation might be able to take them, even temporarily, or knew of a place that could. I spoke with the founder of the sanctuary and the support team who worked with us on a daily basis. We had some acreage in the back of the property, we called it "the back 40", where horses had previously lived, but the area was home now to only three bison.

We determined we could help these horses—for the time being, at least—and try to adopt them out, as horses are expensive to keep. I have never driven a horse trailer, so Martine hooked up her large trailer and headed out for the few-hour trip to pick up the rescued animals. It would prove to be a very long day; the horses were tired, scared, and reluctant to load, which was understandable given all they'd been through.

Fortunately for them, they were in good, capable hands, and were eventually persuaded onto the trailer and brought to the Waystation. I was there to meet them, and found myself shocked at the rough shape the poor things were in.

All four were scrawny and disheveled, and still had the auction house number stickers affixed to their coats. It really hit home for me in that moment that these horses were not considered living, breathing, sentient beings that deserved to live; but instead they were nothing more than products, commodities for purchase from the highest bidder.

The three younger ones were scared, and huddled together after being encouraged off the truck. The older male still had some spirit in him, and stomped his feet, determined to do all he could to let us know he wanted to be the master of his own fate.

He finally allowed himself to be gently led off the trailer by Martine and into the large pen with the others. He joined the others in their huddle, and it was obvious they were all trying to figure out what would happen to them next.

We gave each of them some oats and tubs of water, and they cautiously ate and drank, probably wondering if the food, water, and clean conditions were too good to be true.

Three of the four horses who now call Wildlife Waystation home were unhandled youngsters of only a year and a half; a colt named Orchid, and two fillies that were named Susan and Flower.

Orchid, an interesting name for a male, received his name because he was cryptorchid—meaning only one testicle had descended. Fortunately, this condition has now been remedied thanks to a vet who donated the much-needed expertise for the complicated procedure.

The fourth horse rescued off the slaughter truck was a dark chestnut male named Piute, who was judged to be around three years old. All four were malnourished and full of worms, but with good food and great care they have become fuller, glossy, and downright gorgeous—all thanks to the care of the vets and staff at the Waystation.

I regularly visited the horses in "the back 40", who now get to have the life that every horse needs and deserves. Although it was our initial intention to find homes for them, eventually it was decided that they could spend their days running the fields and enjoying the pastures of Wildlife Waystation.

Feeding, housing, and vet care for all of our rescued animals, including these four, come with costs. If you would like to donate for our work or sponsor an animal please check the website to learn more at wildlifewaystation.org.

᪥◒᪥

Susan Hartland's lifelong mission to protect and save animals began over twenty years ago when she worked with homeless animals in rural shelters. It was through this experience that Susan recognized just how great the need was to stop the suffering for the voiceless. Witnessing this suffering evoked an awareness within her that all animals have feelings and deserve to be treated with dignity and respect; she thereafter embraced a vegan lifestyle. Since then, Susan has served with numerous nonprofit agencies protecting both land and sea animals, and is currently the Director of Animal Rights Netherlands/Belgium.

Until the End of His Days
A Promise to Bear Bear

by Melody Whitworth

It was a cold and rainy afternoon in mid-Missouri. Many of us had gathered at a tiny restaurant in a quiet little town for an annual Valentine Campaign held by our rescue organization, Unchained Melodies Dog Rescue.

Through this campaign, we created handmade Valentines and mailed them to the hundreds and thousands of chained and penned dogs across the country. We had piles of red, pink, and white construction paper, along with doilies, glue, felt hearts, and cute little doggie stickers to create these masterpieces. Our efforts were completed in the hopes that maybe, just maybe, we would pull at the heart strings of an owner or family member who would free their captive dog from a horrific situation.

Suddenly we heard the sound of a vehicle pulling up to the curb. This was not just any car—not a passerby or a volunteer—but a car that we had hoped would come, and our hearts leapt that it had finally arrived.

You see, we had been contacted about a dog—a dog that had been banished to a pen because the family was fearful of him after his guardian passed away. They reached out to our organization instead of euthanizing him, which they'd seriously contemplated, but as it turns out they had made a promise to his owner.

They'd promised they would care for the dog until the end of his days. In the months since his guardian's death, they had strayed from this promise, but reaching out to us was far better than keeping the poor dog in a dirty pen with no shelter, socialization, exercise, or companionship.

Our organization agreed to take him, sight unseen. This dog needed assistance, he fit exactly into our mission, and we were prepared and willing to help him.

We waded through the glitter and paper scraps on the floor and rushed outside to where the car waited along the curb, engine still running. A woman got out of the front passenger seat, and—while leaving her door ajar—whipped open the back door, grabbed hold of a leash, and pulled out a very large, very hairy dog with a massive head.

The woman handed me the leash and said, "Here ya' go; his name's Bear." She jumped back in the front passenger seat, slammed the door, and they sped off without sparing a backward glance for the dog's welfare.

The dog stood frozen, staring at the car's taillights until they became blurry with the rain. He stared and stared until he could no longer see or even hear the vehicle. Even after his "family" was long gone, he sat perfectly still on the sidewalk, his leash slack in my hand.

I imagined what was going through this poor dog's mind, and my eyes watered with sorrow, wondering how someone could do this—leave him without even a goodbye or a look back. I broke the dog from his stare by leading him to my vehicle, where he jumped into the back seat without hesitation.

I moved my hand to pat his back, call him by name, and tell him he was safe and on his way to a better life. Suddenly his body stiffened, his lip curled, and he turned and attempted to bite my hand. Bear had given me enough warning so that there was no contact made with my hand or arm, but I will admit I was taken aback, and I knew then that I needed to proceed with caution.

We had a three-hour drive back to our home from this small town, so we quickly cleaned up the remnants of what was left of the supplies from the Valentine Campaign, packed up, and headed out.

Bear lay in the back seat, staring at me and grumbling under his breath. I knew I had to make friends with this guy or it was going to be a very long ride home. The first fast food joint I came across was a Sonic, so I stopped and purchased the largest order of nuggets they had.

Suddenly it became quiet in the back seat; Bear's eyes softened, his head went up, and his nose was busy with the aroma of the fried food from the restaurant. The order finally came, and I began gently tossing pieces back to him; he moved closer and closer to me, asking for more, until suddenly he jumped into the front passenger seat by my side.

"Whoa, you are a big boy!" I exclaimed with surprise. His eyes were now soft, less suspicious, and he accepted me as a friend, so I hand-fed him the rest of the nuggets until they were gone.

We again set out on the remainder of our road trip, and soon after settling into a steady speed on the highway, Bear laid his head on my leg. He then drifted off to sleep and slept the entire way home. Bear was obviously exhausted, traumatized, and confused, but somehow he had figured out that he was safe, and I continued to assure him that better things were to come.

The next few days were busy ones, with vet appointments, a grooming appointment, and a meet and greet with a foster home which is where Bear would hopefully stay until he was adopted. The foster home that had stepped up for Bear seemed tailor-made for him—a single mom with a young son who wanted a companion.

There was a pond in the back yard for Bear to swim in, and he had a canine buddy that would come over each morning, jump up on the porch, and wait for the screen door to open and Bear to come bounding out for a race to the pond.

Bear became very comfortable in this home, and the family even contemplated adopting him. Then one day, Bear blew it. He made one wrong move, and his perfect foster situation was over.

You see, once some dogs have been isolated and alone, with no "pack" to call their own, they can become very attached, very quickly, to their new family. Sometimes they hold on too tight, and don't want other animals—or humans—to get in their way. The thought of losing yet another family is too much for them, so they go into protection mode.

Bear thought he was protecting the Mother and her son from an intruder coming into their home, but little did Bear know that the "intruder" was a friend who simply wanted to pay a visit to the family—probably even meet this big beast they were constantly talking about.

Bear did the unthinkable in the family's mind and lashed out, biting the man on the hand. I got a call saying, "He has to go, NOW." So I once again put Bear into the back seat of my vehicle and the two of us hit the road.

He'd been so happy, and had such a great life at the foster home, that I couldn't help but mourn for the both of us. Now we needed another plan, and fast.

The search began for a situation or foster that could work

for him. Bear lived with us temporarily while we pursued one idea after another, but every possibility seemed to fall through. People rarely stepped up to foster a boy with these kinds of issues, and we knew it, so Bear would continue to live in our home with us while we waited and hoped.

Bear loved to swim, and he would repeatedly break out of our fence or dart out the door in order to run to the neighbor's pond. When we would go to collect him, he would turn and look at us as if to say "What? A guy's allowed to have a little fun."

Bear quickly became very attached to our family, too, just as he had to the others before us. Unfortunately, Bear continued to do the "unthinkable", and would bite the hands of any "intruders" that came to our door. After some time, everyone that came to our home knew to keep their hands in their pockets!

Bear simply needed to sniff and smell and have some time to know that these people were really family and friends, and were not there to hurt him or any of us.

After a little time with a new human, Bear would throw himself down for belly rubs and all would be well.

There were a few exceptions to this rule, of course. One time an out-of-town guest was staying the weekend, and Bear had decided he was a decent sort of guy earlier in the evening. Late that night, though, Bear was asleep in the kitchen when the friend got up to get a drink and stepped over the dog. Had he never heard the saying "let sleeping dogs lie?" It would prove to be to his detriment.

In mid step, while trying to get to the refrigerator, Bear suddenly awoke and went into protective mode. The dog's head quickly lifted, and within a split second he bit—not the hand of the fellow, but instead right into his gonads. Bear had pierced the family jewels!

Luckily our friend took it in stride, and realized it was his own fault for stepping over a sleeping dog. We chuckled over it the next morning, but it really was a close call, in more ways than one.

Months went by and Bear was comfortable in our home, which was just as well, because there was not one inquiry about adopting or fostering him. He was either too old, too big, too hairy, or sometimes all of the above, not to mention that people were afraid of him once they learned about his protective nature.

Weeks turned to months, and months turned to years, and by now Bear had become family. We grew as attached to him as he was to us.

We loved that crazy dog with all of our hearts, and protected him from his inner demons, putting systems in place to deal with his issues. We always called him Bear Bear, because it seemed fitting and was fun to say in different funny voices.

A few years ago Bear had surgery to remove a tumor from his leg; it was a very difficult recovery, but our boy handled it like a champ. Before we knew it or were ready for it, Bear became older and less sure on his feet, had problems with his hips and back legs, and was on multiple medications to give him relief.

Dementia slowly settled in, and he would walk in circles and lie on the floor and bark at what seemed like nothing at all. Finally he could not get up on his own; yet still we continued to help him up, steady him on his feet, and give him one more day to enjoy a comfy home, love, compassion, and a family.

For you see, we too had made a promise, a promise that we would care for this dog until the end of his days. When the time finally came and our boy left us behind, we stood staring at the homecare vet's tail lights until they became blurry with our tears. We stared and stared until we could no longer see or even hear the vehicle as it crested the hill and passed out of our sight. In the end, it was we who knew the great loss of being left behind, and not Bear Bear, and the irony was not lost on us.

Today we think of him often, and continue to tell the story of the pierced family jewels and giggle as we relate the story. Bear Bear will remain in our hearts until the end of our days and we finally get to hold him again.

ॐ

Melody Whitworth, upon relocating from Florida to Columbia, Missouri, started seeing chained dog after chained dog after chained dog—a concept she could neither accept nor ignore.

Melody is now the President/Director of Unchained Melodies Dog Rescue, whose mission is to rescue, rehabilitate and rehome the chained, penned, abused and neglected back yard dog. Visit unchainedmelod. org to learn more about this fast growing, all-volunteer organization, how you can support them and their mission.

THE ART OF CLICKER TRAINING COWS
Lefty and Friends

BY RHI BANKS

FINALLY FOUND THE PERFECT PLOT of land
'ld Brother Wolf's Animal Sanctuary, it came
ed challenge: a small herd of undersocial-
dy calling it their home.

t what would happen to them if we
nd, and found that they'd be sent to
understood that the lives of those
the lives of the dogs and cats we
day. So when the time came,
contract to buy the land, and

gave them a permanent home to live out the rest of their natural lives.

Before their lucky break, the cows had rarely interacted with humans and weren't quick to trust us. Since they were adults, we knew it was going to take a lot of extra work to get them socialized. But we were up for the challenge! After all, a bulk of our daily work entailed socializing animals of other species, and we were eager to try out some new ideas in our work with the cows.

As it turned out, socializing cows wasn't much different than socializing dogs. We began by simply sitting near them as they ate, and offering them food from our hands. As our presence became more commonplace, we became less of a perceived threat. Slowly, they began to realize that we weren't so scary after all.

Next, we worked to get them comfortable with being handled and taken to other areas for medical care. Inspired again by our work with dogs, we gave clicker training a shot.

Our star student is a 6-year old cow named Lefty. During our ongoing clicker training lessons, we encourage her to touch the end of a long stick with her nose. When she does, we click the clicker and give her a tasty treat. Since she now associates the stick with something positive, she's willing to follow it around. That means we can lead her without having to lay a hand on her, which creates a safer situation for us all. Eventually, we will even be able to use her comfort with the stick to teach her how to walk on a lead!

Not all of the cows are comfortable with us or participating in clicker training just yet, but we can tell that they're curious. They'll eventually come around and we will be ready when they do.

Clicker training has also become a wonderful tool to keep Lefty's brain sharp and active. It gets her thinking What do I have to do to get that treat? Cows are very smart creatures with excellent memories, so it's important to keep them engaged with activities that are more stimulating than grazing all day.

Boredom can lead to mischief, depression, OCD-type behaviors and even self harm, so we like to keep the gears turning inside the minds of these highly intelligent beings. Our team is always learning tried-and-true methods as well as thinking up creative ways to keep the farmed animals happy, healthy, and stimulated.

In addition to providing a safe haven for farmed animals like Lefty, Brother Wolf's Sanctuary, once complete, will provide adoptions, volunteer opportunities, and critical care for dogs and cats who have been so badly abused and neglected that they require longer term, more specialized rehabilitation. The Sanctuary will also be an educational resource for area youth to learn about our responsibilities to animals, nature, and society. Indeed, we intend for the Sanctuary to be a haven and destination for people from all walks of life to connect with nature and our work for the animals. Visit www.bwar.org/sanctuary to learn more!

⊙⊙⊙

Rhi Banks is the farmed animal caretaker for Brother Wolf Animal Rescue. BWAR was founded in 2007 to provide the programs and resources necessary to build No-Kill communities.

FLIGHT OF FREEDOM
Pike the Pigeon

BY JOHNNA L. SEETON

ON A COLD NOVEMBER DAY many years ago, I was film-ing, recording, and documenting the events at yet another Pennsylvania pigeon shoot. Having been to over 100 such "events" in my state, I knew the routine well. In my car, I car-ried all the equipment needed to rescue any wounded birds I might find during, or after the shoot.

What Are Pigeon Shoots?

Pigeon shoots are barbaric contests in which live pigeons are stuffed into small traps on the ground. There are nine traps, which are electronically controlled by an operator, and are situated within a scoring ring on a field. The shooter stands in a certain spot with his or her double barrel shotgun and yells, "Pull!" The operator pushes a button, releasing a single pigeon from a trap. The shooter gets two shots at the bird as the pigeon desperately tries to escape. The scoring occurs if the pigeon lands within the balloon-shaped ring. It doesn't matter if the bird is wounded or dead, as long as he falls within the ring.

It's really as horrific as it sounds.

Many of the wounded birds fly beyond the scoring ring. Hours may go by before the Trappers conduct a "perimeter check." Usually, there are two or three checks during a shoot. Of course, they can't possibly find all the wounded birds; they fly too far away in an attempt to get away from those doing them harm. Any who are found are killed.

We have returned one day, two days, even as many as five days after a pigeon shoot, and we have discovered still more alive, but injured pigeons.

At This Particular Shoot

After six hours of shooting the birds individually launched out of traps on three different fields, the slaughter ended that November day. But my work had just begun. With my net and towel, I started along the public road in pursuit of wounded pigeons. It wasn't long before I spotted a bird huddled in tall grass near the side of the road. I carefully placed the net over him as he tried to flee. Arranging the towel around the net and the pigeon, I returned to the car where the wounded bird was placed in a small carrier. My search continued. I only found one other injured bird that day, and so off we went to the veterinarian's office.

The Veterinarian's Office

Luckily, I had informed my veterinarian I would most likely be bringing wounded pigeons to him. I always let him know in advance when I will be attending a pigeon shoot, and he has agreed to be "on call" in case I find wounded birds. When we arrived, he examined the first bird, "Henry." Henry was barely breathing, and he had many wounds. The vet said Henry was in grave danger, and he didn't think there was any chance of recovery. Poor Henry was humanely euthanized.

Then the vet examined "Pike." He found that Pike was dehydrated and underweight. He decided to X-ray the bird to check for broken bones, internal injuries, and shotgun pellets. Since he was worried about having Pike under anesthesia, he planned to do the procedure as quickly as possible. As it turned out, Pike had four buckshot pellets—two in his right wing, and two in his body.

Fortunately, the pellets hadn't hit any vital organs. The vet administered an injection of Baytril (an antibiotic) and another injection of Dexamethasone (a steroid) to start him on his way to recovery. I had to give Pike 0.25 cc of Baytril orally, every 12 hours. The vet told me to keep Pike very quiet, and to take away the perches in his cage so he wouldn't try to fly.

Pike's Nursing Home

Pike stayed in a large birdcage in my house. I placed the cage by the window, so Pike could see other birds occasionally flying by, and I hoped it would inspire him to get well, too. He did not enjoy taking his medication every 12 hours, but he somehow knew it was necessary, and fought less each time.

I kept classical music playing on the radio for him all day and throughout the evening. He seemed to be healing well and eating, and after one week he went back to the vet for a checkup. The vet was pleased with his progress, and felt Pike's prognosis for recovery was good.

The vet continued the same medications, and told me to maintain the current regimen. Weeks passed, and I could see that Pike was gaining some weight. He was also more active. No longer needing his medication, the vet thought Pike would be ready for rehabilitation in a "flight cage." I knew just the place for Pike!

Moving Day

One of my friends, who also happens to be a veterinarian, runs an animal sanctuary in Chester County, Pennsylvania. He has attended pigeon shoots himself, so he understands the plight of these animals, and has rehabilitated many birds from the shoots. Oh, if only he had room for Pike! Pike was one phone call away from the perfect rehabilitation situation for him, and I was excited and nervous as I placed the call.

The answer was a resounding Yes! My friend would take Pike. I felt happy and relieved.

Yet, loading Pike back into his original carrier for transport to the sanctuary gave me a feeling of sorrow. I knew I would miss him. He was such a sweet, gentle bird, and despite myself I'd gotten attached. But I also wanted what was best for Pike, and I knew he would want to be back with other pigeons. So, off we went from my home in Harrisburg, Pennsylvania to his new rehab center in Chester County.

Flight Cage

When my friend met Pike, he briefly checked him over, and agreed he was ready for the flight cage. He placed a brightly-colored leg band on Pike's leg for identification, so he could recognize him from the other birds in rehabilitation. Entering the barn, I saw three flight cages, all differing in size.

The vet let me take Pike and place him in the smallest, beginner cage. After I gently set him on the ground and stepped back, Pike walked around exploring the area for about a minute. Then, he tried to fly, actually making it about a foot off the ground!

I wanted to scream "YIPPEE!" but instead I quietly said, "good boy, Pike." By the time I was ready to leave, Pike had flown to the lowest perch (about three feet off the ground), which was excellent progress for his first day.

Pike was now with other pigeons. I hoped he would be happy, and I left there sad for myself, yet eager for forward progress for the sweet bird I'd grown to love.

The Next Step

I called my friend every other day for the next two weeks. Each time I was told that Pike was making great progress, and getting all "A's" on his pigeon report card. I was ecstatic. He had moved into the third and largest flight cage, and had pretty much mastered all his necessary skills. The vet thought in about a month Pike would be ready to be placed in a covered outside cage in order to prepare him for his final step—FREEDOM.

The month passed slowly for me. I now called the vet once a week to check on Pike, and finally, the day had come for Pike to be transferred to the outside cage! I drove to Chester County to watch him reach his next milestone.

What a beautiful outdoor cage! As with the other flight

cages that were inside the barn, this cage housed many pigeons who were on their own individual paths to liberation. When the vet brought Pike out to his new home, he immediately flew around with the others, one step closer to a normal life for his kind.

Pike stayed in the outdoor cage for about a month, during which time I went back to see him twice. I was relieved he had the leg band, because by now he was one of the flock, and I would have had a hard time identifying him without it. I felt proud for him, and ecstatic to have this happy ending for both of us.

At last, the day came for Pike's freedom flight: the vet opened the cage door! This allowed the pigeons to leave the cage, return if they felt they needed to, or fly freely!

I watched Pike anxiously, half wanting him to go live his life, but worried for him, too. Pike didn't venture beyond the cage that first day while I was present. It took Pike an extra week to leave the fenced confines, and then he and some of the other pigeons would return "home" for food each day.

My friend told me some of the pigeons never leave, they just fly in and out of the cage, using it as a nesting grounds of sorts. Pike did this for about three weeks.

Then, the day came that he no longer returned. Pike finally had his freedom! That dear, sweet bird was free.

I've rehabilitated many pigeons under a veterinarian's supervision during my years advocating on behalf of these birds. Pike was my favorite, and still holds a piece of my heart. I even had an image of him tattooed on my arm, because I will never forget my sweet friend, or the plight of the pigeons.

☙❧

Johnna L. Seeton is a retired Pennsylvania schoolteacher who has worked on bills against pigeon shoots for 32 years. She spent time protecting animals as a humane society police officer, and attended over 100 pigeon shoots from 1986-2012, often rescuing injured and dying birds.

Pennsylvania, as of this writing, has still not passed a bill protecting pigeons.

EVERY DOG DESERVES A CHANCE
Doogie, Loved by Many

BY TAMIRA THAYNE

The End

I WAS AT MY END. I writhed in the dirt, unable to stand, knowing this day would likely be my last. I wondered: is this really all there is to life? A chain, a backyard, a paltry doghouse, and a goodbye that mattered to no one?

It would seem that way.

I'd counted two sunrises since I could no longer stand, yet no one living in the warm house, out of the rain, had bothered to help me or even come see if I was still alive.

A neighbor watched from her window as a frigid September drizzle worked its way through my fur and onto my skin. I could hear her moans, and thought maybe she was hurting too. A man came out her front door and cross to my owner's door. He pounded, then talked very loudly, pointed over at me.

Finally, my owner approached. Would he help me now? Could there be an end to the pain?

He took me by the collar and roughly yanked me up, speaking to me in harsh tones. I cried out, as new waves of agony swept through my spine. He put me into a sitting position and walked away, yelling at the man to go home.

I fell over, a whimper escaping my clenched jaws.

It was not to be.

Soon, my family came out of the house: the woman, the man, the son, and his friend. Hope again clutched at my desperate heart. They talked and laughed as they loaded up the loud little cars and left, sparing me not a glance.

I lay on the wet ground, the flailing of my head carving

a notch into the grass as I tried in vain to stand. The white dog—also on a chain—and the little dog in the pen eyed me anxiously, but could do nothing to help me.

We all lived as prisoners, yet longed to be pets.

The neighbor who moaned was here. She held a bowl of water to my mouth, and I drank greedily. Even when I could stand, the cool liquid was hard to come by, and I often drained puddles left by the rain. She still moaned, soft sobs ripping from her throat and coating me in sadness.

She hand-fed me soft morsels of dog food, and I lapped fervently at her hand, taking all she had and wanting more. She talked softly as she worked, telling me help was on the way—she'd called the emergency police, and she promised they wouldn't let me suffer any longer.

But no one came.

I waited as the day slipped into night, still mired in my rain-soaked cavity on the ground. Her gifts of water and food had given me energy and hope, yet both waned as darkness fell.

Finally, my family came home, laughing and joking as they put their vehicles away and went into the house, again sparing me not a glance.

I was invisible.

The third sunrise broke, and with it another light but relentless rain. My family all left the house early, forgetting me, as I suffered in silence on their lawn.

The Middle

The woman moaned at my side. I was so cold I shivered, and I had no interest in her offerings of water or food today.

What was the point of drawing out my ending? I had no desire to go on.

The woman's promises of help fell on deaf ears; her weeping became louder, and she hovered over me, not knowing what else to do.

She finally staggered back to her home, leaving me to rest in peace.

Just as the last remnants of my faith in humanity were slipping into the dank mud beneath me, help arrived in the form of two strangers and a van.

They saw me.

The women rushed to my side, checking to see if I was breathing. I kinda wanted to know the answer to that too, but my pain told me that, unfortunately, I hadn't yet passed to the other side. Surely doggie heaven could not hold this much hurt.

The moaning woman left her window and hastened to

our little gathering, and the one in charge asked her if my owners were home. They were not.

They talked to me with hushed but kindly voices as they decided what to do.

Finally, they removed my collar, lifted me gently onto a blanket, and carried me to the van.

It was warm inside! And there was no rain. Already hope wormed its way through my empty soul and into my heart.

The women drove me straight to a doctor, where they met a man who must have been the animal police. He was not happy that the women had taken me from my soggy prison, and lectured the boss woman as they all eyed me from the open hatch of the van. I raised my head as much as I could and stared back at them.

Couldn't he see that I needed help?

The woman stood her ground, telling him I had to have

immediate vet care, and if he wanted to be the one to assist me, then here I was—he was more than welcome to get me the relief I needed. He grumbled some more, but then picked me up and carried me into the vet's office, informing the woman to call him later.

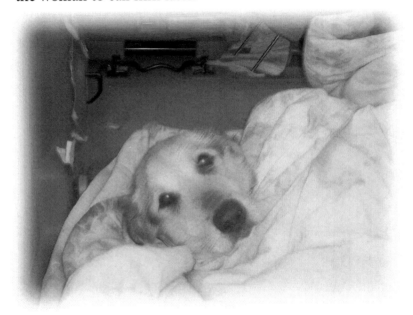

The doctor and nurses were so kind to me. I might have cried if I were able, as this many people hadn't paid attention to me in many, many years—if ever. My rescuers told the doctor what they knew, which wasn't much, and they did tests to see what was wrong with me.

Finally, the woman asked the doctor what should be done. His response? "Every dog deserves a chance."

I was given some shots of medicine and vitamins, and some more medicine to take with me. The two women carried me back out to the van, and we traveled in the warm vehicle to our next stop: a place with other dogs and lots of barking.

They carried me inside and straight to a tub, where I was given a bath—the water was warm at least!—and the mud and feces were washed from my fur. As a dog, I wasn't too sure about the fancy smell, but I had to admit it felt good to be clean again. Or, for the first time in my very long memory.

Between the medicine, the bath, and the plentiful food and water, I was starting to feel like a real canine again. I lay on a soft blanket by a heater, and a couple friendly dogs were allowed to come and make my acquaintance. Once I felt safe and warm, I put my head down and dozed peacefully.

Maybe everything would be ok.

∽∾

It wasn't long before my ears perked back up. The rescuer in charge was talking on the phone, and she sounded upset. What was happening now? Was my safety all an illusion?

Soon a man came to the house, a friend of the woman's. The boss spoke to him in urgent tones, and I was carried to a small car. The man was nice, but I felt the shattering of my newfound tranquility. Maybe there really was no promise of a happy ending for me; maybe I needed to come to terms with it.

Maybe I was just unworthy of love…

∽∾

We drove around all night, to different places, as the man spoke with a low-pitched but strained voice to the people he met. After many conversations and a few stops, he found me a place I could stay, where I was inside, seemingly safe for the moment, and warm again.

I slept the dreamless sleep of the exhausted.

By the next morning I experienced a miracle. I could stand! Even though it was still painful for me, my muscles had begun to work again, and when I started my morning flail, suddenly there was a difference: I was able to push myself off the floor and climb shakily to my feet.

When the humans came to check on me, they were surprised to see me up and walking about the room. They smiled and laughed, patting me on the head and feeding me dog treats as they gently led me outside for a bathroom break.

I'd already done most of my peeing in the room (which I

would later learn was a no-no), but I had enough gas in the tank to mark a few bushes and trees. They seemed satisfied with that, and praised me for what I saw as my duty.

In the next week, my life held no stability, although I would take this nomadic path each and every day over what I'd left behind. I was not bored, and I could shuffle along on my own, so I was moving in a paw-sitive direction.

I changed locations a few times, and each occasion brought me another human who was kind to me; each giving me tasty morsels, fresh clean water, and pats on the head. I slept inside the homes with these new people—which I'd never been allowed to do before—and gradually learned to save my pee and poo for outside time.

Apparently the humans frown upon defecating in the house. Live and learn.

Even though I could still walk, I started feeling worse again once the shots of vitamins and painkillers had left my system. The pills the humans gave me hurt my belly, but I was unable to let them know, so I resorted to the only means I had to tell them something was wrong: I tried to bite them.

TV crews had started to come around, and the people I was with told me I was now a doggie celebrity. This was new to me, and since I wasn't feeling well, not a particularly welcome addition to my life—although I could appreciate the irony of going from invisible to VIP in the span of a single week.

After I tried to bite the TV anchorman, my rescuers knew I needed to go back to the doctor again, and so I took another, this time much longer, trip.

I was finally at the place I would come to know as home.

The Beginning

My belly hurt, and I was grumpy. So grumpy that I didn't want humans or dogs around me, and I'm ashamed to say I'd lash out when they came near. There was another woman at this new place, but I didn't pay her much attention, because it seemed there was always another woman, another man, and I'd decided not to get attached.

Plus, I just didn't feel good.

The next sunrise saw me at another doctor with the new woman. This doctor did more tests, and then once again gave me some shots that brought me a welcome and instant relief from my suffering. The pills that hurt were exchanged for different ones, and the new medicine didn't hurt my tummy—which made me a happier dog.

I stopped trying to bite people, especially the woman I was starting to think of as Mom.

Who was I—without the pain, without the chain? I wasn't sure I knew.

I'd been at this new place for a week, when I started my transition from "the grumpy room", aka the garage, to the inside of the home with Mom and the other dogs. I liked it.

Before long the boss woman who picked me off the ground and took me to the doctor came to visit. I admit that I showed off a little, flaunting my now-sleek black and tan fur, gobbling a yummy snack, and then running up and sticking my nose in her camera lens.

I was feeling my oats, what can I say! I really didn't know this lady, but I knew that my life had changed the day she and the other two women took a chance on me. That was good enough for me.

I now had a mom for the first time in my life, and other doggie companions by my side. Yes, I still had arthritis and back pain, but the pills helped me get up each morning and delight in each day. Mom fed me a high-quality diet, even cooking for me and making sure I had delicious and nutritious meals.

I had a yard to run in, and lots of bushes and patio furniture to explore and pee on. (I still had my duty to attend to after all.)

Most of all, for the first time ever, I knew the real meaning of love, and a freedom from chains that I'd never before experienced. Maybe I was wrong before. Maybe I did deserve love, and maybe that first doctor was right.

"Every dog DOES deserve a chance."

Thank you to everyone who gave me that chance.

—Doogie

NOTE:

Although the author uses her imagination in describing how Doogie would feel were he able to speak for himself, what happened here is indeed a true story.

Doogie's rescue and subsequent court battle shocked animal lovers across the country. The evidence of abuse was overwhelming, yet authorities did nothing about it. In fact, they did the opposite, charging the dog's rescuer with criminal acts, while treating those who left Doogie to die as victims.

FACTS OF THE CASE:

Tammy Grimes (now Tamira Thayne), dog rescuer and founder of Dogs Deserve Better, was arrested September 11, 2006, for helping a dying chained dog in East Freedom, Pennsylvania.

That dog was Doogie.

She was charged with theft, receiving stolen property, trespassing, and criminal mischief.

The District Attorney offered Grimes a plea deal, which stated she must return the dog to those who abused him in exchange for her freedom from prosecution. She refused.

She then had to scramble to find a safe place for Doogie to live out what remained of his days.

The Doogie hearings would drag out for almost a year and a half. Charges of trespassing and criminal mischief were quickly dropped, but Tammy was ultimately convicted of misdemeanor theft and receiving stolen property, and sentenced to 300 hours of community service for a "people" organization—because, according to the judge, "people are dogs too."

Grimes requested jail time instead, but was refused. The judge would not allow the jury to view the video of Doogie chained and unable to stand. She allowed only photos of the rescue, some of which are pictured here, but the video is what depicts the true extent of Doogie's suffering.

Grimes lost her appeal, and was refused a hearing for a pardon by the Pennsylvania Board of Pardons. Her actions in rescuing and caring for Doogie ended with her carrying misdemeanor convictions on her record for ten years.

The video of Doogie the day of his rescue is available at this link on YouTube: https://youtu.be/YN9t1rv4pj4

You can also watch the video of Doogie at his foster mom's home five weeks later: https://youtu.be/TlUToFd_dwQ

The trial itself lasted three days, with dog advocates packing the courtroom. Activists also demonstrated multiple times outside the courthouse throughout the many months of back and forth courtroom drama.

The vet gave powerful testimony on the stand, telling the District Attorney and the jury that the dog was indeed suffering, that he needed help, and he deserved a chance at life.

But in the end, none of it mattered. The judge instructed the jury that as long as Grimes admitted to taking the dog—which she did—the reasons for her actions didn't matter. The jury deliberated for only 30 minutes before returning a guilty verdict.

Doogie lived another five months with his new mom, and she loved him dearly. She's the only person who got to know the "real" dog beneath the pain and the chain. Tamira remains grateful to her to this day. Kathy truly went above and beyond, putting herself in harm's way to minister to a dog in need.

Words from Doogie's Rescuer and his Dog Mom

OPEN LETTER FROM TAMMY GRIMES
AFTER HER CONVICTION:

On September 11, 2006, I rescued a dog who was dying at the end of a chain in a muddy yard in a small Pennsylvania town. I was subsequently arrested. A little over a year later, on December 14, 2007, I was convicted of theft and receiving stolen property.

The last year has been the most traumatic and the most inspirational of my life. I have been labeled a "terrorist", a "vigilante", a "publicity hound", and an "anarchist." I have been called a hero. I have been humbled by encouragement and well wishes from people all over the world. I have been attacked in person and in print in my small town, where the prevailing view is that it is just fine to tie a dog to a tree or a dog house and leave him or her to pace for year after agonizing year, in skull-cracking cold or 100-degree heat, with nothing but parasites for company.

I don't regret what I did. Not for one second. Here's why.

The dog at the center of all this, a dog we would eventually name Doogie, had been lying in the mud and rain for three days, chained to the dog house he had been attached to for most of his life. He was unable to stand and was pawing the air in desperation.

His owners chose to go four-wheeling all weekend and to work on Monday instead of getting him the vet care he needed and deserved, but most importantly was entitled to by law. A distraught neighbor called animal control repeatedly over the course of the three days. But as so often happens, no "humane" officer called back. No one ever showed up. (Surprised? Trust me, it happens all the time, and not just in my town.) The frantic neighbor eventually reached out to me and to Dogs Deserve Better.

What I did next set in motion a chain of events that would eventually garner national attention, the wrath of some, the support of others, and an agonizing trial during which I had to listen to lies and mischaracterizations for three days: I removed that dog's chain and I took him to the veterinarian.

It was all very clear to me as we lifted the emaciated, wet dog into my van. I had been in animal rescue long enough to know that I would probably be labeled the villain while the dog's caretakers wouldn't even be questioned for leaving a suffering dog on the ground the way he was.

But I also knew that what I was doing was morally correct. It was the compassionate thing to do. It was the only thing to do. Time was of the essence. A dog was suffering. I believed he was dying.

In court, it became increasingly clear that our "humane" officer left me holding the bag, which in this case amounted to a bag of bones. Instead of getting an arrest warrant for Doogie's owners—as he'd promised me he would after seeing the dog's condition and carrying him into the vet's office— he took no action outside of telling the police that I had the dog and lying about it in court.

So, now I'm guilty...guilty of caring about a dog that had been left to die. Guilty of putting myself, and my reputation, on the line because I couldn't stand to see his suffering. Yes, call me guilty.

Doogie blossomed after we got him medical care and showed him a warm bed and a little love. He not only walked again, but actually ambled about with a spring in his step. Imagine. A dog that for many years could not take more than a few steps before being yanked back by a chain, was trotting around a yard and enjoying soft hands and a warm home!

The support I have received during the last year has made me stronger in my convictions and more steadfast in my work. I know that the vast majority of reasonable, educated, compassionate people believe that it is barbaric beyond imagining to chain a dog for life. I know that anti-tethering laws will continue to be passed in states, cities, and counties across this country. (A recent news article called these law "No-brainers.")

Oh yes, make no mistake: times change and morality and compassion eventually triumph over ignorance and stupid, blind habit. Slavery ended. Women got the right to vote.

I can't help but think about Rosa Parks. We can be sure she never regretted refusing to budge from that Montgomery bus seat. And though I may never make her mark on history, I'll never regret taking a half-dead dog from someone's yard in order to help him.

In memory of Doogie. May he rest in true peace, knowing he was indeed loved—and seen—in the end.

—*Tammy S. Grimes, December 17, 2007*

FINAL WORDS FROM A DOG MOM:

It's with great sadness in my heart that I tell you that Doogie passed away yesterday morning (March 1st) around 9:10 am.

Doogie had surpassed all goals I had set for us both. He learned how to smile, love, kiss, hug, wag his tail, trot (yes! literally trot!) up to me and check me with his hip in an attempt to play. He gently took food from me and never complained about anything we had to do to help him.

I thank you, Tammy, for letting me have time with him. He was an amazing little old man and sadly, the way he lived, no one enjoyed his comedy; a life spent chained had done a number on his mind. I have had much training; I studied animal behavior, first aid, and thank God I live in a place where cruelty charges would have been brought and upheld on the owners of Doogie for the condition I saw him in—and that was after weeks of care.

I want to thank everyone for the presents Doogie received and all the well wishes. Please know he went very peacefully and on his own; he chose his time and was not in any noticeable pain. I hugged him and told him all the amazing stories about the bridge, about how people who have hurt him will suffer in the end, and about Tammy's amazing love in refusing to give him back to an immediate death.

Doogie had five months with me, during which time we both learned so much about love. People would thank me caring for him, but in the end it was he who gave me the best gift of all—the gift of knowing and loving him.

—*Mom, aka Kathy*

☯

Tamira Thayne pioneered the anti-tethering movement in America, forming and leading the nonprofit Dogs Deserve Better for 13 years; her swan song culminated in the purchase and transformation of Michael Vick's dogfighting compound to a chained-dog rescue and rehabilitation center.

She is the author of *The Wrath of Dog, The King's Tether, The Knight's Chain, The Curse of Cur, Foster Doggie Insanity, Smidgey Pidgey's Predicament, Happy Dog Coloring Book,* and *Capitol in Chains.* She is the editor of *More Rescue Smiles,* and the co-editor of *Unchain My Heart* and *Rescue Smiles.*

Tamira now lives by a river in the woods of northern Virginia, with her husband, daughter, one dog, six cats, and hundreds of outside birds and critters she adores from afar.

STREET CROSSING 101 FOR RESCUERS
Turtles Deserve Better

BY JOSEPH HORVATH

LET ME START BY SAYING THAT not all stories have happy endings. This one does, but sometimes in order to experience that happy ending you have to experience sadness along the way first . . .

And it's not a story about saving a dog, either, or any of the usual companion animals. Instead, it's a story about how I learned that all animals, not just dogs, do matter.

My girlfriend at the time, Tami, and I were driving to Florida to surprise her best friend for her engagement party.

I had rented a cherry-red convertible Mustang for the trip, so we put the top down and were running 80 mph in the center lane of I-95—which, as you can imagine, was quite an enjoyable experience for a lover of speed such as myself.

Now, I understood that Tami loved animals, but I didn't understand until this trip just how much. As I said, we were cruising down I-95 when we passed a turtle attempting to cross the six-lane highway; not such a smart move on his/her part.

I was instructed (yes, by Tami) to stop and go back.

Ok, she may have yelled it at me but then the top was down so she probably had to, right? It took me about 1/2 mile or so to get stopped and over to the side of the road. I backed up and backed up until we were a mere 100 feet from saving this poor misguided turtle . . . but as it turned out we were 100 feet too late.

A sadistic trucker decided today was the day he was going to take out an innocent creature, and so he deliberately ran over the turtle, which at the time was on the dotted line and should have been safe.

Tami was devastated. She could not stop picturing that poor turtle, and she asked me to catch up to the offending trucker so she could give him a piece of her mind. As we pulled alongside him, Tami uttered a significant amount of choice words to the driver (with associated hand gestures), and I vowed no turtle would die on my watch again.

☙❦

Fast forward to six weeks or so later and we are again rolling down the highway, although this time it's a four-lane divided road heading out of D.C. We're less than a mile from the traffic light when I see a turtle in our lane, attempting to cross.

Feeling more confident in my duties this time, I spring into action by immediately slamming on the brakes and pulling over without so much as a sideways glance at Tami. As I'm backing up, I see the light change and two lanes of traffic begin to accelerate toward the turtle. I decide today is not his (or her...I mean really, how can you tell) day to die, as memories of Florida flash through my mind.

I throw the van into park, jump out, and grab that turtle, getting us both into the median right as the two lanes of traffic come hurtling past. After traffic clears on the other side, I carry the turtle across the remaining two lanes and over the guardrail, taking him (or her...I mean really) down to a little creek.

Now, I will admit I may not have scoped out the whole situation thoroughly when I grabbed that turtle, and so I'm feeling pretty good about my save when I get back to the van—that is, until Tami asks me which way the turtle was heading.

She then forcefully reminds me that you have to carry the turtle off the road in the direction it's heading, or he or she will just turn around and go right back into the road again.

Now, I will also admit that I might have made some assumptions in regards to which way he (or she . . . I mean really) was going. They are round, right? It's not like they are shaped like an arrow.

I assumed the turtle was ONE lane into crossing the four-lane highway. I didn't take the time to consider that he or she might have been THREE lanes into crossing the highway and I put him (or her) back at the starting point.

That possibility could earn me the wrath of Tami.

I'm going to stick with my gut feeling on this, and emphatically state that the turtle was at the start of the journey and I truly did save him (or her...I mean really) a whole lot of footwork and a possible early demise crossing that highway.

It's what lets me sleep at night.

Turtles Deserve Better, after all.

∽

Joseph Horvath is retired U.S. Air Force, and works as a government contractor in the D.C. area. He still rescues turtles from his driveway and has been known to yell at the local bears.

A Gift for an Elder
Wolfie's Last Foster Home

by C.A. Wulff

"The wolves knew when it was time to stop looking for
what they'd lost, to focus instead on what was yet to come."
—Jodi Picoult, Lone Wolf

I met Anne in the autumn of 2017. She was a resident of the skilled nursing facility where my lifemate had been admitted for rehab after a stroke had taken away her motor skills. Every morning I would drive the short distance to the facility and spend two hours helping my partner work through her exercises. There were almost always other residents receiving therapy at the same time, and often one of them would be Anne.

I was enchanted by the tiny Italian woman who wore flowers in her hair and pranced on her feet like a nervous pony. She didn't always remember us from one day to the next, but she was darling, and we looked forward to seeing her.

Around dinnertime, I often drove back to the facility to help my partner with her meal and stay to visit for a little while. For these early evening excursions, I usually brought one of our five dogs along for added comfort for my partner. The dogs quickly got into the groove and enjoyed seeing all the residents and getting some extra attention.

I would learn that a good many of the residents had dogs they had left at home, and they missed these companions very much. Anne would light up when she saw our dogs, and would tell me stories about the four Maltese she'd been blessed to live with.

Over time, I found out that Anne was a ward of the state: she had a court-appointed guardian, and when she'd been put into a nursing home in 2013, they had taken away her last remaining dog and placed him into a foster home. His name was Wolfgang Amadeus Mozart, named for Anne's favorite movie, Amadeus.

The last time Anne had seen Wolfie was two years earlier on her birthday.

Her story and the circumstances surrounding the loss of Wolfie pulled at my heart strings. I couldn't imagine being locked up somewhere I didn't want to be and unable to spend time with my dogs.

On Anne's good days, she would dote on our dogs and walk them around the halls of the facility. She told me over and over how much she missed her Wolfie, and my heart broke for her each time. His caretaker lived more than an hour away, too far to bring him for visits.

Right around this time, my friend, LeAnn, asked me to read a business proposal she had written for one of her college classes. It would be a moment of cosmic synchronicity: the proposal was about helping the elderly who could no longer care for their pets. Was it a sign that I needed to do more to make things right for Anne and Wolfie?

I talked it over with my lifemate, and we agreed that we could foster Wolfie at our house if I could get in contact with Anne's guardian and work out the details. Since we lived so close, we'd be able to take him up to see Anne a couple of days a week, and, our plans finalized, I couldn't wait to run the idea by Anne. Once she got over the initial shock that virtual strangers were willing to help reunite her with her dog, she was over the moon with excitement.

When I approached the nursing home administrators about our plan, I was told there were rumors that Wolfie was sick and dying. Deflated, I tried not to get my hopes up too high, but I moved forward with our course of action anyway. The nursing home helped me reach out to Anne's guardian, and from there to the woman who was fostering Wolfie.

In less than a week, we had set up arrangements to meet to discuss the situation and Wolfie's needs. The much-anticipated meeting went off without a hitch, and it turned out I'd been worried for nothing. Anne's guardian readily handed over Wolfie and all of the little guy's earthly possessions to me; in fact, they seemed almost eager to pass him along to a new foster situation.

From there, we drove straight to the nursing home to bring Anne and Wolfie back together again, and the joy I felt at seeing the two of them made all the planning and headaches surrounding it worthwhile. For the first time in years, Anne got to spend the afternoon with her dog, and I got the gift of witnessing their happiness.

In the end, the rumors of Wolfie's imminent demise had been greatly exaggerated. He's been our foster dog for ten months, and Wolfie has settled into our home with our other dogs and our daily routine. He sees his mama, Anne, two or three days a week, and I get to love on him and enjoy his infinite cuteness the rest of the time.

Fostering Wolfie has not been without its issues—no good deed and all that—but we've been working through them the best we can. His physical challenges have improved with research and a change of diet, so today I'm feeling pretty positive in that area.

Behaviorally, though? Well, there was the "not-answering-to-his-name" issue, and the "won't-sleep-through-the-night" issue, and let's not forget the ongoing "barking-&-whining-

because-apparently-he-likes-the-sound-of-his-own-voice" issue, too.

We have our good days and bad, like everyone, and once in awhile I have to remind myself that I willingly signed up to be Wolfie's foster mom—and that I did it with very good reason. If I'm still struggling to remember, I simply drive him to visit Anne, and then I remember all over again.

My gift to Anne has turned into a gift for all of us. Life is good.

☙❧

C. A. Wulff has been involved in pet rescue for over twenty-four years, volunteering with Ohio humane group Valley Save-a-Pet. An author, artist, and animal advocate, Wulff uses her art and writing to spread the joy of the human/canine bond. Her books, *Born Without a Tail: the Making of an Animal Advocate* and *Circling the Waggins: How 5 Misfit Dogs Saved Me from Bewilderness,* chronicle her personal journey of animal rescue. Her books *How to Change the World in 30 Seconds* and *Finding Fido.* are guides for animal advocates and pet parents. You can follow her on her blog "Up on the Woof", where she shares biscuits of dog-related info. [thewoof.wordpress.com]

Wulff currently resides in one of our nation's National Forests with her lifemate and five dogs. She attributes her love of animals to having been raised by Wulffs.

KITTINSPIRATIONS TO US ALL
Braillie and Cassius

BY DARLA PURGASON

Braillie

SOMETIMES THE WORLD IS A DANGEROUS PLACE for our fur-covered friends. People use poisons on their grass to kill weeds; cars and trucks leak oil and anti-freeze all over parking lots. There are innumerable ways that these and other toxic chemicals can reach the animals.

Cats who live outside, unfortunately, often walk through these toxins and, as we all know, they then lick their fur and paws to stay clean. Whatever they walk through can end up in their stomachs due to this desire to stay neat and tidy.

Just like human mothers, what affects an animal mom will also affect the babies. Braillie's mom must have gotten into something awful, because every kitten in the litter was born with eye problems.

The whole family had been rescued by our group after being tossed from their home by an elderly guardian who could no longer care for them. One kitten had "baby doll eyes", so that when you tilted her head back, her eyes would blink closed, just like a doll's.

Sweet little Braillie was born blind; she had no eyes at all, just the sockets where her eyes should have been. She had her mother's coloring, with medium-length gray hair, white on her chest, and little white boots on her feet.

Because Braillie was blind from birth, she knew no other world, and thought being blind was normal. If awards were given for fantastic cats, Braillie would certainly have won one. Even without the ability to see, nothing stopped her from chasing her toys that jingled or rattled, using her litterbox, playing with other kittens, or even jumping up onto her foster mom's bed at night to snuggle.

Braillie used her front paws to check out her environment. She sensed where we were in the room, and would follow us around or turn her head to follow movements in her vicinity. Just think how sensitive her hearing and smell must have been!

Nothing scared her. She went everywhere with a cheerful, happy attitude, no matter how noisy things got. She would just lay back and enjoy the people and attention all around her.

Braillie's first "forever home" fell through when the lady's cat didn't like her. Then her perfect home came along: a retired couple asked to adopt her, and the volunteers at Animal Allies worked with them so Braillie could visit schools and nursing homes.

After all, if anyone could serve as an inspiration on living your life to the max, even with a disability, it was Braillie.

No vision? No problem! She's just happy to be here.

Cassius

How many of you remember the times you didn't obey your mom, and you ended up paying a price for it? Mothers try very hard to care for and protect their babies, but youngsters don't always pay attention or follow Momma's instructions or advice. Cassius was only four weeks old, but he thought he knew more than his momma.

He wandered away from the cozy den she'd built for him and his littermates, and fell smack down into a drain!

He couldn't get out, and his mom couldn't get to him either. Poor little Cassius cried and cried, and the longer he was there, the louder he cried. Finally, a nice man heard all the noise from inside his office, and went outside to see what was going on. There was Cassius, stuck down inside the drain, and looking quite the pitiful sight.

The nice man was a dog lover, but he couldn't just walk away and leave poor ol' Cassius stuck like that. So he got some tools and took the drain apart to reach the stranded kitten. Cassius' face was all scratched from his head-first fall, and he wanted his mommy, badly. Although he mewled and hollered for her, she wouldn't come out to get him, because she was a homeless cat and afraid of humans.

There was nothing the nice man could do but bring Cassius home with him to his family. The family put him in their kitchen in a great big box, checked the internet to see what to feed such a small little guy, and then called Animal Allies for help.

A volunteer with the organization went to their home to pick up the kitten, and had only driven a few miles when she realized the kitten was ill. He was taken straight to the vet, who pointed out that Cassius not only had a cold, he was also full of fleas. He was given medicine and taken to a foster home where he could recuperate from his ordeal.

Cassius was an orange tiger kitten with white markings. On his front feet, the white markings looked just like the white tape on a boxer's fists. He was also really feisty, just like a prize fighter, and every time his foster mom came into the room he would attack her feet and hands. Yeah, it was funny when he was a kitty, but probably wouldn't end up so funny if the behavior continued into adulthood!

Cassius found a loving home along with another homeless kitten. As it turned out, he'd met his match, because the other kitten was named Cheddar, and she was much larger than Cassius. They fought and rolled around at first, but in the end she taught him to back off and mind his manners. He would still get wild and crazy every now and then, zooming through the house and up and over the furniture, but Cheddar just gave him the stink-eye, letting him know she wasn't impressed and he needed to settle down.

The scratches on his face from his scare as a baby healed nicely, and left no scars. I'm sure if his momma could speak to him, she'd tell him if only he'd listened to her that day, he wouldn't have been hurt. Sometimes Momma really does know best!

〜〜

Darla Purgason is retired from her work in Washington, D.C., and keeps busy with cat rescue endeavors as well as caring for her own four beloved long-haired kitties. She enjoys trying new vegetarian recipes, listening to books on tape, and doing embroidery. She is the author of *A "Tail" of Two Christmases*, and makes her home in Culpeper, Virginia.

AN UNEXPECTED ENCOUNTER
Finding Ferret

BY LIZ WOLOSKI

IT WAS A BALMY SUMMER EVENING when my husband Al and I were driving home from the city, the backseat laden with grocery bags. As we traveled down the highway, I was staring absentmindedly towards the far, west-bound lane that was under construction, when something caught my eye.

A strange undulating animal of some sort had risen from the ditch and was loping along its edge and around barricades and traffic cones. Leaning forward, I peered around my husband, who was driving, for a better view.

"What's that?" I pointed in the direction of the unknown creature.

"Where?" He glanced sideways.

"Over there. That animal! Look!"

"Weird," he squinted again. "It looks like an otter."

I craned my neck to look back as we motored past. The animal was now scampering back into the long grasses in the ditch. "It can't be an otter," I said. "There's no water around here for miles. Quick, turn around. We have to see what it is."

Al glared at me. "What? How am I going to do that? Didn't you see all the construction work? That lane is covered with barricades."

"I know, but you can get around them," I said. "You're good at that sort of thing."

He sighed heavily, that familiar sigh of resignation I knew so well. "Why do I listen to you?"

At the next opportunity he turned the car around and we headed back, Al maneuvering through wooden stands and around traffic cones.

"This is nuts," he said.

"Over there!" I pointed. "I saw him! He ran down into the ditch."

Al steered the car through a set a of barricades and up an approach onto the frontage road, then turned off the ignition. We sat for a moment peering through the windshield, when suddenly the critter popped up from the ditch and stood on its hind legs on the road before us. "That's a ferret," I said. "I bet someone has dumped it."

It is a sad fact that there are cruel people who drive their pets out of the city limits and release them when they are no longer wanted. Never understanding why they were deserted, the betrayed animals run along the roads trying desperately to find their way back home. We had seen abandoned dogs and cats before, but a ferret was something new.

"I think you're right," Al agreed. "It does look like a ferret."

"You need to catch it," I said.

"Catch it?" My husband turned to me wide-eyed. "It could be wild."

"Well I can't do it," I said. "I'm wearing shorts and sandals. I have no protection at all if it bites."

"But what if it has rabies?" he said.

"We can't just leave it here," I shrugged. "The poor thing will never survive. I'm going to get it." My hand went to the door handle.

"Oh, for crying out loud." Al opened the driver side door and stomped out. I leaned across the seat for a better view and watched as he took a leery step forward, holding his hand out towards the ferret, an animal we were unsure was feral or tame or possibly rabid.

The weasely creature took one look at Al and charged towards him. *Oh no*, I thought. *That does not bode well.* Then I heard Al yell, "It ran up my pant leg!"

Oh dear.

I watched with mild amusement as my husband stood shaking his leg, finally managing to extricate the critter from his pants. Hurriedly he opened the back door of the car and flung the ferret on top of the grocery bags.

We drove off in silence as the animal wound its way

through the white plastic grocery bags, slithering through the hand holds like a snake. I gathered my legs under me and sat on my feet, praying he or she didn't venture to the front seat.

"Something stinks to high heaven," Al announced, adjusting the rear-view mirror and scowling through it for a view of the backseat and the obvious source of the odor. The smell was noxious; a musky, skunky stench that permeated the vehicle's interior.

"It's just a little stinky," I said. "I'm sure the scent will disappear once we let the car air out." But secretly I wondered if the stink was now embedded in the upholstery permanently.

As we turned off the highway and down our gravel road, the ferret continued to bounce wildly around the back seat, through the grocery bags and up onto the back-window ledge, and then down onto the floor and back up to the ledge. He only seemed to have one speed—and that was full blast. There was no telling where he would go next.

"I just don't want it to leap on my head," I cried, attempting to cover my head with my arms.

"Well you're the one who made me catch it!" said Al.

And then there it was, on the floor in front of me, staring at me with its beady little eyes and razor-sharp teeth. "Please don't bite me," I mouthed. It must have sensed my fear because suddenly it darted back under the seat.

Minutes later, we were grateful to arrive home, tense and anxious to get out of the smelly car. I opened the door and as I began to exit the vehicle, the ferret leapt out in front of me and raced across the lawn to the edge of our property, where a colony of Richardson's ground squirrels made their home.

In seconds he was fiercely clawing the ground and flinging dirt in the air.

"No!" I screamed. "Come back. Don't you dare hurt the squirrels!" I loved that our little acreage was a haven for birds and wildlife. Now I felt as though I had unleashed a serial killer into my bucolic, peaceful neighborhood.

As I started towards the squirrel colony, the ferret must have decided he had had enough of squirrel digging because he abruptly stopped and made a beeline back to us. He flew across the lawn like a torpedo, zipping between our legs and up to the front door, where he finally stopped and turned to look at me as if to say *what are you waiting for, open the door!*

"I believe he wants in the house," my husband commented.

"He's obviously tame," I said. "And kind of cute too, but there's no way he can come inside. Who knows what bedlam would occur with the dogs and cat if they see him."

"Not to mention his aroma," Al added.

It was decided, that for the time being, the ferret would be relegated to the garage. As I bent over and placed a tentative hand under the furry rope-like body, the creature immediately dove down my neckline, under my top and ran laps around my rib cage. I whirled about madly, shaking my bosom like a show girl until the critter popped its head out and I was able to reach in and yank him out. Grasping him firmly with both hands, I quickly made my way to the garage, opened the door and thrust him inside.

He sped off to explore these new surroundings, racing along my husband's work station with its tools and automotive devices, then over to an old roll of carpet and stack of household items readied for the goodwill. I sniffed my arms and drew back. I had to have a shower already—the stink was pernicious.

Shortly after, our ten-year-old daughter Kim arrived home from her friend's house. She was naturally excited to see the new creature in the garage. We prepared bowls of cat food and water and made our way to the garage.

"Don't let him out," I warned, slowly pushing the garage door open. Quickly we slid through the doorway and closed the door behind us.

I had expected the usual frantic race in our direction but there was no ferret to be seen and the garage was deathly quiet. "Here Stinky!" I called as we set the bowls on the workbench. Where was he?

"Come out, little ferret guy!" Kim shouted. For a moment we stood listening and peering around the garage. Could he have somehow escaped? We each began searching; under the lawn tractor and behind pieces of machinery, amongst gardening tools and a stack of folding lawn chairs. Then Kim peered into the carpet roll and said, "I see him!"

There he was, stretched out in the tunnel formed from the rolled up rug. But he wasn't moving. "Stinky! Wake up!" I said, jiggling the carpet back and forth.

"C'mon, Ferret!" Kim called. I grabbed the bowl of food and waved it at the entrance of the carpet tunnel hoping the aroma would arouse his senses, but to no avail. He laid in the carpet, deathly still. As I rolled the carpet back and forth, his weasel body remained inert, rolling flaccidly with the carpet.

He's dead, I thought. He must have gotten into something in the garage, though I couldn't imagine what. I'd rescued the poor creature only to send him to an early death. I should have brought him into the house. What kind of a horrible person would just throw a helpless animal into their garage like that?

"I think he's waking up, Mom!" Kim said as she peered down the upholstered burrow. "It looks like he's opening his eyes."

Yay! I didn't kill him after all!

He blinked and yawned, slowly returning to the land of the living before crawling out of his cozy den to greet us. Tentatively, my daughter put her hand out to pet him. Stinky immediately fled up the sleeve of her jacket, sending her into fits of laughter, and I knew all was right with the little guy.

Kim spent hours in the garage with this new creature, bringing him treats and cat toys to play with. The next morning, alarmed that he wasn't in his carpet tunnel and unable to find him in the garage, she called for me in a state of panic. We had to search for him all over again.

After turning over almost every item in the garage, I happened to look up to see a sleepy-looking ferret face peeking over the edge of the canoe that was tied to the rafters.

He was fun to play with, curious and comical and always very busy. But I knew we could not keep him. Ferrets are not solitary creatures—they need at least one other ferret to keep them company, and the garage was no home for a living being. Living in our house was out of the question; our inn was already full, with dogs and cats and birds and a rabbit.

I called the Humane Society, on the off-chance that someone had lost their ferret. The lady I spoke with informed me that nobody had reported a missing ferret, but if I wanted to surrender him they would certainly find him a good and loving home. There were lots of people out there who adored ferrets, she assured me, and would certainly want to adopt him.

We were all sad to have to say goodbye to the little fellow. I felt horrible putting him into the cat carrier for the trip to the Humane Society, but I knew it was the right thing to do. At the reception desk everyone made a fuss over him, so I was somewhat relieved knowing he would be in good hands. "Bye, ferret guy," Kim said, stroking him one last time.

In the end, it was a good thing we surrendered the ferret when we did. The next day when my husband went out to the garage to start the lawn tractor, all the tires were flat.

Turns out they like to chew, and the little stinker had chewed off all the valves stems on the tires.

Oops, sorry hun.

ᎾᏪ

Liz Woloski is an animal lover and lives with her husband and two dogs in a small town in Manitoba. She's written on and off all her life and hopes to devote more time to writing now that she's retired.

AN OLD DOG'S VALUE
Zena's Inner Light

BY JOE MARINGO

IT WAS A BITTER COLD JANUARY DAY, just like most January days at the Hillside SPCA in Pottsville, Pennsylvania. The temperature was hovering right at zero in mid-afternoon. Even so, cars and people were coming and going. Dogs were barking and playing in the snow. Staff and volunteers were attending to the chores of the day. Little did anyone know that two things would happen on this frigid afternoon that would change the lives of several people and one very special dog.

First, a news crew from WNEP-16 in Scranton arrived to do a story on the frigid temps and the many area dogs who were forced to spend their days and nights chained outside.

Second, as the crew was setting up in the adoptions office of the shelter to start their interview, a car pulled into the lot and a well-dressed man came over to Liz, one of the humane agents there. "I'm here for my appointment," he told her.

Puzzled, her reply was "What do you have an appointment for?" She hoped maybe he had come to adopt a new companion or find out how the adoption process worked.

Sadly, that was not the case at all. "I have an appointment to have my dog put to sleep."

This really confused Liz, since Hillside is a no-kill facility. "I'm sorry, but we don't euthanize animals here, we're a no-kill shelter."

It turned out the man and his family had made an appointment with another shelter some distance away, but had driven here by mistake. "Well, can you just put her to sleep for me?"

Again, Liz told him, "As I said, we don't euthanize dogs. If you want that done you will have to drive to the shelter you have the appointment with."

"Well I'm very busy and don't have time to drive all the way across the county; and besides, I've missed my appointment now. Can I just leave her here with you?"

"If you would like to sign her over, we will take her in and try to find her a new home."

"Well, I don't know who would want a seventeen-year-old dog, but you're welcome to her. Where do I sign?"

Liz had him fill out the surrender form and went with him to get the dog out of the car. When he opened the door, one of the saddest old dogs Liz had ever seen literally fell to the ground at her feet. She looked at the form the man had filled out for some info on the dog.

The dog's name was Zena, she was seventeen years old, and she had spent her entire lifetime on a chain. While the man, his wife and kids drove off in their warm, comfortable car, Liz gathered the old arthritic dog up and helped her toward the office.

The news crew had just gotten their equipment set up and turned on the camera to check the settings when a sobbing Liz came through the door. It was fate, or a divine hand that told the cameraman to keep filming.

"He just opened the door and she fell out at my feet," Liz sobbed loudly. The other staff jumped into action, wrapping Zena in blankets trying to warm her up. "She's been chained out for 17 years. This is probably the first time in months she's been warm!" That was the lead in to the story about bitter cold temps and dogs forced to live outside on the six o'clock news in Scranton that night. It was also my introduction to the Hillside SPCA and to the heroine of this story.

My friend Julie always sends me interesting pictures, stories and internet links. She is particularly fond of the Hillside shelter. When she saw the story online later that night, she just naturally sent it on to me. Not knowing what to expect I clicked on the "WATCH VIDEO" link. The first thing I saw was the staggering old black dog with the white muzzle, and Liz sobbing and telling her story. I was only ten seconds into a two-minute video and I was crying right along with them.

Next, I saw them in the office offering her a bowl of food. The dog seemed confused, and it was then that I noticed the dog did not seem to have any eyes. It looked like she just had two empty sockets. The video went on to talk about other dogs and cats living outside in the freezing cold, but all I could see was the old black dog. The odd thing I remembered was the sheer look of joy on her face at just the slightest attention people were giving her. A warm blanket and a kind touch made her face light up with pleasure. I emailed Julie right away to let her know that she had once again brought this big tough guy to tears.

There was no sleeping that entire night. The anguish that Liz felt for the plight of this gentle soul, and her smiling white face filled my mind instead. At 8 a.m., I eagerly wrote up another email to Julie, "I'm calling Hillside when they open. If she is still there, I'm adopting that black dog!"

The shelter website said they opened at eleven that day, so at 11:01 a.m. I was on the phone. I had met their other Humane Agent, Janine, once about a year earlier. Janine was on the video as well, so that is who I asked for when someone answered the phone. A few seconds later Janine was on the line. It is much easier talking to someone you know, even if it was just a brief meeting, so I was happy to hear her voice.

"Hi Janine, this is Joe from Southwest Pennsylvania Retriever Rescue, do you remember me?"

"Well sure, how are you doing?"

"I'm doing great, but I have a question for you. Do you still have that old black dog that was on the news video last night?"

"Yes we do, why?"

"Is anyone interested in her? I assume you have had a few

calls with the publicity that story got."

"No, not a single call. You're the only person who has even asked about her."

This absolutely broke my heart. How could others not have been moved by what they had seen, as I was? Had the world become so callous as to not even care about an old dog?

"Well Janine, would you like to place her in a happy forever home?"

"ARE YOU SERIOUS! Are you considering her?"

You could hear the excitement and thrill in her voice, along with just the slightest hint of pleading. "It would be my honor to let her live out the rest of her life here with me and my family."

The rest of the call was a bit frantic. There was a thud and I could here Janine yelling in the background "SOMEONE WANTS HER, SOMEONE WANTS TO ADOPT ZENA!" Janine put Liz on the phone and I got all the important info about Zena. She was seventeen years old, had spent all or most of her life on a chain outside, she was very stiff with arthritis and had a hard time walking. She was also totally blind and probably deaf as well.

Now to most people these health problems would have caused them to have second thoughts about adopting Zena, but not me. I didn't hear one thing that gave me any reason to question my intentions. My mind just kept going back to her smile—as long as she had that, everything else was minor. Liz and I talked for a few more minutes and I told her I would make the 600-mile round trip three days later.

I spent the next three days just like a proud parent, sending pictures and the video link to all my friends. I also posted her pictures and info on the three Labrador chat forums of which I'm a member. The response was as I expected, hundreds of people and friends sending best wishes for Zena and their thanks for saving her. A few people even said they were also moved to tears, and that they were going to try to help dogs or shelters in their own area as a result.

Tuesday morning dawned sunny and clear for the first time in days. The thought of driving to the Poconos with the potential for bad weather was the one thing that could have thrown a wrench into my plans. I warmed up the truck, loaded up my best buddy Blacky the Labrador, and headed east. The trip was pretty routine. As always, Blacky, who is my heart-dog and constant companion, lay quietly on his bed in the front seat, his head on my lap.

Halfway there I had a flash of inspiration. I called WNEP-16 in Scranton to see if they were interested in doing a follow up on the original story. The lady I spoke to said they might be able to get a camera out, but since the new president was being sworn into office today, the news crews were pretty busy. Someone would call and let me know if they could make it or not. The call never came.

About 1:00 p.m., I pulled up the steep road to the shelter. The lot was filled with cars and some were even parked along the road. I managed to squeeze into a spot next to the cat building, which was good since I had also brought a large donation of cat food for the shelter. When I got out of my truck, I was surprised to see an SUV from WNEP-16 there. They had gotten the cameraman from the first story to come down and film the happy ending. We shook hands and made our introductions; then, with cameraman in tow, I set off to find Janine.

"Hi Joe, how was the trip?" Janine asked, big grin on her face.

"Long, but worth every minute and mile."

"Would you like to meet your girl?"

"I sure would! I'll follow you," and off we went. We entered a small office, and there lying on a dog bed in the corner was Zena. People have asked me what I thought when I first saw her, and my reply was "She's dirty, smells bad, her hair is falling out in clumps, she's blind, deaf, arthritic, and without a doubt the most beautiful girl in the world!"

Of course, it didn't matter to me how she looked or smelled—just that her smile was still there. I bent down to pet her, forgetting that she was blind and deaf, and my touch startled her, but just for a moment. She quickly realized I was there to pet her and sat up, leaning firmly into me. Before I knew it, she was ROO-ROOING in delight while the camera caught it all on tape.

After a few moments, she stood up and started walking in circles around me. This greatly surprised the staff, as they had hardly seen her walk in the days since she had arrived. Then came the real surprise: she walked over, licked my face, let out a small bark, sat down, and offered me her paw. It caught me off guard, and I didn't have a chance to receive it before she had to put it back on the ground to steady herself. They filmed a bit longer and then we went outside for a short interview.

Zena walked down the hill to my truck to meet Blacky. Blacky is a very good boy, and while he is afraid of most people, he never met a dog he didn't love. We had a few pictures taken of me, Zena and Blacky, then it was time to head for home. I thanked the cameraman for doing the original story with Zena in it, and Janine for taking Zena in and allowing me to adopt her.

The ride home found me answering my cell phone every few minutes. Everyone wanted to know if I had her and if she was as sweet as she seemed on the video. My answer was, "Yes, she is even SWEETER!"

Once we arrived home I offered her some food, water, threw another log in the fireplace, and set out several dog beds for her. I didn't know if it would be too warm for her thick fur, so I put beds all over the family room for her. Again, she surprised me by picking the one only three feet from the fireplace and falling quickly asleep. The next morning, eight hours later, she was still in the exact same place. Zena was finally home.

One week later, Zena was fitting in like she'd lived here for years. The other dogs all loved her, and my wife Barb loved her too. Zena's contagious smile has moved to my face now. Every time I pet her, or walk her, or even just look at her, I find myself grinning from ear to ear. Perma-smile is what they call it I think. Each day she has become a little stronger and a little more steady on her feet.

We have found that she can hear, at least a little bit. She will come if I whistle, and she can without doubt hear the sound of kibble falling into a stainless food bowl. She barks if she needs out to potty, and she has a pretty good memory of the family room and front yard. Unfortunately, there will be no happy news about her eyes, as they are beyond repair.

Our wonderful vet, Dr. Bowser (yes, what better name for a vet!) says it was probably Glaucoma that was left untreated and the pressure caused the eyes to rupture and atrophy. No matter though, because blind dogs see with their hearts! That is so true, because whatever Zena lacks in other areas, she makes up for in heart.

I think back now to her supposed caretakers saying "Who would want her?" and I am profoundly sad. Not for Zena, because she now has all that a dog, companion, member of MY family could ever ask for. I feel sad for her former family. For a man who could not see the value of a dog, the love that waited to be shared at any moment with just a kind touch and a scratch under the chin. For the wife who did not shed a tear for the faithful friend who had spent seventeen years with her family.

But the saddest part was the cold lesson those kids learned that freezing January day. When something gets old, when the toy has lost its shine, you just throw it away. I wonder how these kids are going to handle their parents when they become old? Maybe the same way the parents dealt with Zena?

They said there is no value to an old dog; well I say they have it all wrong. To me, Zena is a priceless gem, a jewel, a diamond that I am proud to add to the safe deposit box that is my heart.

Joe Maringo is the Director of Southwest Pennsylvania Retriever Rescue Org/S.P.A.R.R.O. and Shades of Grey Sanctuary For Senior Dogs in Plum, Pennsylvania. Over the years SPARRO has grown and to date they have rescued over 1,000 dogs, from every single state east of the Rockies and from Canada as well. Learn more and donate at sparro.org.

Thank you for Joining Us in the Celebration of
More Rescue Smiles. We Hope You Enjoyed the Book!

COULD YOU TAKE A MOMENT TO GIVE IT
A SHORT REVIEW ON AMAZON.COM? YOUR REVIEWS
MEAN THE WORLD TO OUR AUTHORS, AND HELP THEM
EXPAND THEIR AUDIENCE AND THEIR VOICE.
THANK YOU SO MUCH!

Find links to *More Rescue Smiles* and all our great books
on Amazon or at www.whochainsyou.com.

ABOUT THE EDITOR

Tamira Thayne is the author of *The Wrath of Dog, The King's Tether, The Knight's Chain, The Curse of Cur, Smidgey Pidgey's Predicament, Happy Dog Coloring Book, Foster Doggie Insanity,* and *Capitol in Chains.* She is the editor of *More Rescue Smiles,* and the co-editor of *Unchain My Heart* and *Rescue Smiles.* In 2016 she founded Who Chains You, publishing books by and for animal lovers, activists, and rescuers.

In her empathy for the plight of the chained dog, she pioneered the anti-tethering movement in America, forming and leading the nonprofit Dogs Deserve Better for 13 years.

During her time on the front lines of animal activism and rescue she took on plenty of bad guys (often failing miserably); her swan song culminated in the purchase and transformation of Michael Vick's dogfighting compound to a chained-dog rescue and rehabilitation center.

About Who Chains You Books

LOVE ANIMALS? WELCOME! OUR BOOKS APPLAUD ANIMALS AND THOSE WHO CARE FOR THEM, STAND UP FOR THE ANIMALS, AND CELEBRATE THE CONNECTION BETWEEN HUMANS AND OUR NON-HUMAN FRIENDS.

At Who Chains You, we publish books for those who believe people—and animals—deserve to be free.

We seek to educate, entertain, and share gripping plights of the animals we serve and those who rescue and stand in their stead. At our deepest levels, we explore what chains we humans must break within ourselves in order to free the animals.

Read more about us at whochainsyou.com.

Also from Who Chains You Books

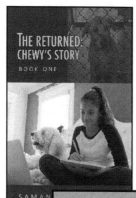

Also from Who Chains You Books

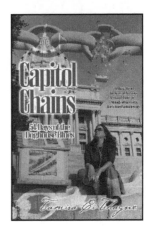

And More!
whochainsyou.com

Also from Who Chains You Books

THE DOG THIEF AND OTHER STORIES
BY JILL KEARNEY

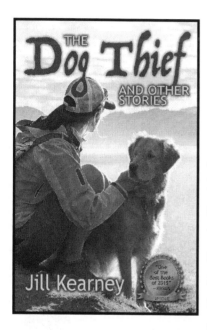

"**D**ecrepit humans rescue desperate canines, cats and the occasional rat in this collection of shaggy but piercing short stories."

Listed by Kirkus Review as one of the best books of 2015, this collection of short stories and a novella explores the complexity of relationships between people and animals in an impoverished rural community where the connections people have with animals are sometimes their only connection to life.

According to Kirkus Review: "Kearney treats her characters, and their relationships with their pets, with a clear-eyed, unsentimental sensitivity and psychological depth. Through their struggles, she shows readers a search for meaning through the humblest acts of caretaking and companionship. A superb collection of stories about the most elemental of bonds."...*Read more and order from whochainsyou.com, Amazon, and other outlets.*

Also from Who Chains You Books

FOSTER DOGGIE INSANITY: TIPS AND TALES TO KEEP YOUR KOOL AS A DOGGIE FOSTER PARENT BY TAMIRA CI THAYNE

Have you ever fostered a dog—happy to make a difference—but wondered why you felt frustrated and alone in your experience? Do you want to foster a dog, but don't know where to start, how to prepare, and what to expect? Have you experienced burnout or compassion fatigue in your rescue experience? If so, this is the book for you. Described as "an embrace from a friend who understands what we all go through; it is a beacon of hope to let other rescuers know they are not alone—a must-read for anyone involved in rescue."

This is not a book about dog training, but a book about people training while working with dogs...*Read more and order from whochainsyou.com, Amazon, and other outlets.*

On the far side of the Olympic Peninsula in Washington State, halfway between the mountains and the ocean, stands the little town of Forks. In that town, in a quiet neighborhood of modest homes and shabby businesses, there remains a dilapidated pink warehouse.

Packed inside that warehouse, living in deplorable conditions, were once over 120 dogs. Some of the dogs were kept in crates piled high on shelves, arranged in rows along the walls, and shoved into corners behind heaps of garbage and urine-saturated straw. Some of the dogs were confined to wire-sided or glassed-in kennels. One was kept in an old horse trailer. Dead ones were stored in a cooler.

In one of the crates was a black dog named Daisy. This is her story. It is also the story of the rescue of 124 dogs—and one snake—from the Olympic Animal Sanctuary...*Read more and order from whochainsyou.com, Amazon, and other outlets.*

Made in the USA
Middletown, DE
12 September 2018